Detangling the Web of Life

The Complete Guide to Understanding YOU and Everyone Else

Ally Ammo

First published by Ultimate World Publishing 2023
Copyright © 2023 Ally Ammo

ISBN

Paperback: 978-1-922982-86-5
Ebook: 978-1-922982-87-2

Ally Ammo has asserted her rights under the Copyright, Designs and Patents Act 1988 to be identified as the author of this work. The information in this book is based on the author's experiences and opinions. The publisher specifically disclaims responsibility for any adverse consequences which may result from use of the information contained herein. Permission to use information has been sought by the author. Any breaches will be rectified in further editions of the book.

All rights reserved. No part of this publication may be reproduced, stored in or introduced into a retrieval system, or transmitted in any form, or by any means (electronic, mechanical, photocopying, recording or otherwise) without the prior written permission of the author. Any person who does any unauthorised act in relation to this publication may be liable to criminal prosecution and civil claims for damages. Enquiries should be made through the publisher.

Cover design: Ultimate World Publishing
Layout and typesetting: Ultimate World Publishing
Editor: James Salmon
Cover image copyrights: Sugarless-Shutterstock.com

Ultimate World Publishing
Diamond Creek,
Victoria Australia 3089
www.writeabook.com.au

Dedication

This book is dedicated to *difference*; those who live it, feel it, think it and especially the courageous souls who strive to make one. The world needs you (and so do I)!

And to Ben... for reasons ;)

Note from Author

Dear reader,

This book contains sensitive and potentially triggering content that you may find distressing or unsettling. It's important that you make an informed decision about your reading experience so before you begin, please note that the following themes will be explored:

- Abuse (physical, emotional and sexual)
- Violence
- Addiction
- Eating disorders
- Mental health challenges
- Trauma

Please exercise self-care and discretion while reading. The FREE Mind Magic Resource has activities and exercises in it that have been specifically designed to support your self-care while reading the content in this book. (QR code found in chapter 1.) This valuable tool was created in collaboration with professionals so rest assured that we've got your back!

However, you should also be aware that pseudonyms have been used to safeguard the privacy and confidentiality of all individuals involved. This decision was made out of deep respect and careful consideration for those that have graciously shared their stories with me.

Contents

Dedication	iii
Note from Author	v
The First Thread	1
Chapter 1: The Web of Life	7
Chapter 2: Understanding Cycles	21
Chapter 3: Element 1: Beliefs	33
Chapter 4: Element 2: Relationships	43
Chapter 5: Element 3: Experiences	55
Chapter 6: Element 4: Environment	69
Chapter 7: Element 5: Childhood	81
Chapter 8: Element 6: History	97
Chapter 9: Element 7: Energy	111
Chapter 10: Element 8: Science	123
Chapter 11: It's All Connected	135
Chapter 12: It's Time to Break the Cycle	147
Acknowledgements	163
About the Author	165
Mind Magic Resource	167
Speaker Bio	169
Sure-Fire Strategy Session	171
References	173

"The **web of life** is a tapestry of relationships, woven from the threads of our actions, thoughts and emotions."
- Deepak Chopra

"There is a **web of life** into which we are born, and from which we can never fall."
- Jack Kornfield

"We are all interconnected in the **web of life**, and our actions have a ripple effect that extends far beyond ourselves."
- Bryant McGill

"The **web of our life** is of mingled yarn, good and ill tied together."
- William Shakespeare

"The **web of life** both cradles us and calls us to weave it further."
- Joanna Macy

The First Thread

Have you ever tried to figure out who you are and how you came to be that way? When we self-reflect we do so subjectively, in that there are always feelings and opinions involved. When we do our best to look at our whole lives objectively and focus on the facts, the past inevitably comes up. And as soon as your past is brought to the surface you cannot help but feel. Flashes of memories run through your mind, feelings rush through your body and before you know it - you're on an emotional rollercoaster.

Life is enough of a rollercoaster as it is, so jumping onto an extra one you didn't line up for can be difficult to get off. Sometimes it becomes impossible to avoid. Maybe you feel nostalgia for all the good times - the monumental experiences, the meaningful relationships and those beautiful moments that made life worth living. You might be grateful simply because they happened and love the feelings that arise on the steady incline that pulls you to the peak. Or, you might find yourself longing for that old joy ride on Magic Mountain over the Tower of Terror you're on now.

Running through the highlight reel of the past can remind you of how far you have come, but it can also show you that you aren't living with thrills and giggles anymore. Chances are though, the main memories that pop up aren't the ones that create a fuzzy feeling frenzy, but are the deeply scarring events that rocked you to your core. Now comes the series of unexpected big dips, twists and turns that make you have to hold in the contents of your stomach. All the pain, anger, resentment, regret, shame and guilt from the past speeds up this ride. With your heart racing, breath shortening and hands shaking - you want to get off. Now! Screw this! Damn them! And stuff this emotional roller coaster I somehow ended up on… again!

I wonder if you, like many of us, struggle to stop the past coming up in the present? Your mind keeps circling back to memories of events that hurt you. As soon as pain is pulled to the surface you realise you don't have a clue how to deal with it. With no time and no tools, you intentionally distract yourself and push it back down. Maybe like me, you cut ties with the toxic people in your life in an attempt to heal and put your past behind you. Yet you found that time and distance have done nothing to stop your deepest wounds from repeatedly being exposed, to you and anyone around.

You want to stop reacting to certain situations based purely on your emotions, but it's like your internal processes have been set in concrete. And I'm sorry to say it - they have. Even the ways you try to cope with difficulties are cemented.

Unfortunately, our go-to strategies often cause us more problems rather than provide any solutions. I know from experience that life's stress can quickly cause a relapse on behaviours and addictions you thought you had long left behind. Everything from denial to drugs immediately numbs the pain of an unwanted experience, though the relief is short-lived.

The First Thread

You get a break in the moment, but you're just avoiding the problem and ultimately compounding it in the long run. How you coped in the past then becomes your biggest challenge in the present. You may be living with anxiety, stress, sleep issues, addiction, depression, self-doubt, denial or constant triggers. You get frustrated that you are back in the same place, doing the same thing, facing the same problems and are dumbfounded as to why.

> *"We can't solve problems by using the same kind of thinking we used when we created them."*
>
> *- Albert Einstein*

You know something major needs changing and you want to make that happen, but where do you begin? It all starts with your perspective! The Web of Life unveils a new outlook that is simple, practical and relatable. Having an objective view of your life will empower you to process and accept your past, giving you the freedom to finally let it go. This method of self-discovery will help you understand your challenges and forgive yourself for any mistakes you made along your journey. The Web of Life can create an easier pathway to forgiveness of others too, but it begins first with the self.

Through new eyes and a unique perspective you can understand yourself with clarity like never before. So no matter how complicated your past and problems seem right now, this powerful and life-changing shift will make sense of your life experiences fast. You can easily uncover all that lies beneath your surface, revealing the negative cycles that keep you stuck in life. You will see how you unconsciously allow them to continue and be given all the crucial tools and tricks to liberate you from repeating them. This will boost your personal growth and potential to break the cycles for good so you can live the free and happy life you deserve.

It can be a lifelong journey to know yourself and understand what makes you *you*. In July of 2016, I eloped in Bora Bora, Tahiti. I had manifested my dream of jumping into the Pacific Ocean in a wedding dress and I felt on top of the world. But unfortunately, when I left heaven I went straight back to hell. The family dramas and relationship difficulties continued once we returned home, so I spent the next year unhappy until the marriage ended. I was relieved it was over, but wanted to grow through my new-found freedom.

In the past, I would focus on the negative aspects of the other person and what they needed to change to improve their life. This time I wanted to focus my energy on revealing this about myself. You see, I'd always been misunderstood. It's confusing and frustrating when no one really *gets* you because you constantly question who you are and everything you do. During this time I realised that it was my true self that I needed to get to know. I didn't need the acceptance of others, just a deep and compassionate self-understanding.

How could I discover who I truly was while processing my past? After searching online I came up short. Everything that was suggested I was already doing. Now I'm sure most of you have heard that we must *journey within* to find all the answers. The problem is we don't really get what it means and we have very little clue how to do it. Wanting to know yourself is amazing, but without a simple formula for self-discovery you are likely to give up and keep it on the to-do list.

I had often heard about the Web of Life but couldn't find it anywhere. Turns out it was just an abstract concept that didn't actually exist, so I decided to bring it to life. Early in 2018, the Web of Life was born. I quickly learned that not only had I found a way to make complete sense of myself, but to easily understand anyone.

CHAPTER 1

The Web of Life

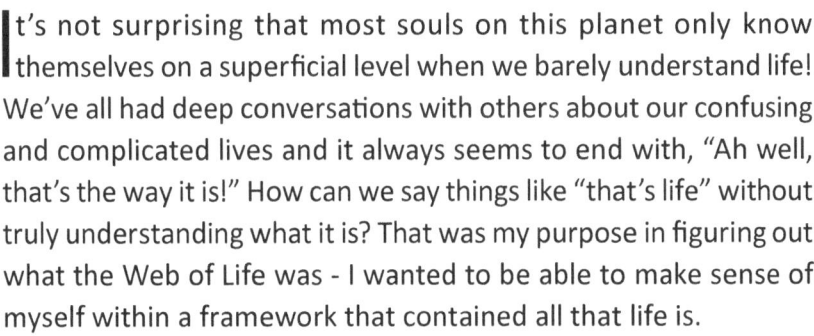

It's not surprising that most souls on this planet only know themselves on a superficial level when we barely understand life! We've all had deep conversations with others about our confusing and complicated lives and it always seems to end with, "Ah well, that's the way it is!" How can we say things like "that's life" without truly understanding what it is? That was my purpose in figuring out what the Web of Life was - I wanted to be able to make sense of myself within a framework that contained all that life is.

It was hard to understand who I was without recognising the outside influences that greatly impacted me. It was also impossible not to account for the events (good and bad) that helped mould me into the person I am. By isolating these factors I created the eight fundamental elements. The self-doubt within me battled for months as to whether or not I had the right pieces put in the right places for the puzzle to come together. So my true measure of success was seeing if other people could understand themselves with the Web of Life.

Since 2018 I began introducing it to people from all walks of life and its impact was *instant*. People had epiphanies, profound insights and life-altering aha moments as they could understand themselves and their lives for the first time. When anyone told me their life story I would weave their web in front of their eyes and watched with wonder as it resonated with them, as if on soul level.

Afterwards I was always asked if they could take the Web of Life home with them, so I realised it is a highly valuable and powerful tool. I know it has the potential to create positive and transformative changes for you too. Don't worry, you automatically gained FREE ACCESS to a PDF called the Mind Magic Resource with everything in the Web of Life when you purchased this book.

This resource will help you cement the shift in your perspective and boost your personal growth. It is the companion to this book and includes fun activities to learn the Web of Life philosophy, journal writing prompts, mindfulness colouring pages, as well as meditative and creative exercises to fast-track your journey of self-discovery, recovery and mastery. Just scan this QR code to download yours now!

The real beauty of the Web of Life is that you can begin to understand yourself simply by looking at it. So don't be surprised if your mind immediately and instinctively begins to make connections.

The Web of Life

"When we change the way we look at things, the things we look at change."

- Wayne Dwyer

A New Way of Seeing

Whereas spiders weave a geometric masterpiece, our webs look like a tangled mess! No wonder we get stuck when we're all caught in our webs for life. It makes sense to think that the ties to our pasts can never be undone, feel like our focus on living in the present always gets twisted and believe we cannot unravel a better future.

This philosophy allows you to take an introspective and reflective new perspective on your life. It's the simplest and easiest way to understand all that you are and break through the limitations on everything you could be. You are so special and unlike any other person on the planet because you are the *only one* with your unique combination inside your web. Every spider's web is as original as your fingerprint - and so is your Web of Life!

We try to make sense of ourselves based on what happened to us and how we got through it, but we're always left with questions as to why and how it even happened in the first place. This is a method of self-discovery where you can begin to understand yourself by uncovering all the major influences that shaped you.

You are comprised of your beliefs, relationships, experiences, childhood, history, energy and the science behind it all. Each one of these fundamental elements combine to form the sum total of your reality. This is the basic structure of your Web of Life.

Now you may be in the centre of it, but it didn't start with you at all! As you will soon discover, your web had begun to be woven even before you were born. So no matter your challenges in life, this new way of seeing yourself and everyone around you can change everything. Life may feel like an inescapable entanglement but you *can* detangle your Web of Life!

The Eight Fundamental Elements

The eight fundamental elements are the greatest influences on you. Together they have shaped who you are, created the path you took, and formed the way you think, feel, act and speak. As you detangle your Web of Life using these elements, the obstacles you repeatedly face will make sense because you will see how they're connected to the past.

Knowing what lies inside each of your elements is crucial as it explains the outcomes and experiences of your life. This will guide your understanding of where your perception of reality actually came from. Only then can you choose what to hold onto and what to let go of.

Empowered with this perspective you can create an entirely new reality for yourself. You will unlock your full potential so you consciously construct your web for the first time in your life. You may have felt like you've been going around in circles, but soon you will be equipped to weave a web of wonder.

The beauty is that you can use the Web of Life to understand anyone as the eight elements are fundamental to all of us. They hold the secrets to understanding everyone you know too. You will find you connect more genuinely, deeply and readily with others knowing that we are all entangled in our own webs.

Detangling the Web of Life

As different as we all appear to one another from the outside of our highly complex lives, it is obvious that we are all connected by the Web of Life. We only differ from one another in the details woven within our elements. It is easy to detangle the web of another, just like it is easy for you to point out the flaws in someone else. But it is important to use the web to know yourself completely before you use it to truly understand anyone else.

To grasp the deep connection between the eight fundamentals, you must know that no element stands alone. There are four strands that make the Web of Life. Each element is linked to its counterpart and shares the same strand in the web. Did you notice that environment is connected to relationships or that beliefs is tied to history?

There is an intricate dance between the two elements that share a strand. Flick back and have another look. The two fundamental elements on one strand are directly tied to one another. For example, you can't think about your relationships without considering the environments in which they took place, and your environments are just physical spaces without the relationships you have within them; including your relationship with nature. You cannot focus on one element without the other coming up.

Your family history influenced the beliefs that were introduced to you, so they are both connected. Your personal history has created most of your beliefs. So as you explore each element in your web, you will find that the one opposite has the greatest influence on it.

How can you talk about your childhood without sharing your experiences? When you tell a friend about a recent incident with a family member, you will always find that experience tied to a memory from your childhood. How can you talk about energy without connecting it to science? Science covers our understanding about everything, and everything is energy. It is also difficult to explore each strand without considering the other three. They are all as connected to each other as you are to your web.

The Core of You

A spider's web is fragile enough to be torn down in a storm, yet strong enough to hold a spider. It's incredible how something so delicate can also be so structurally sound, just like you. A spider weaves a web starting with three main anchor points that make a Y shape and create a supportive foundation. Your Web of Life begins the exact same way and is anchored by the same three points.

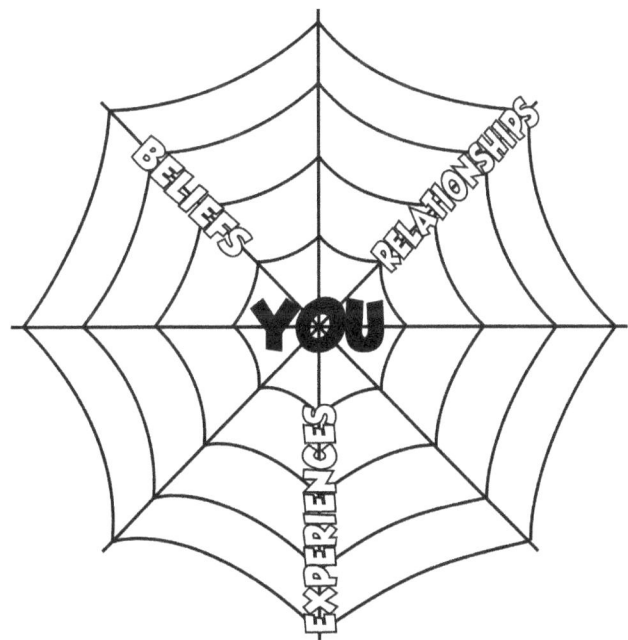

These elements are the core of you and your web. Collectively they play a monumental role in your life and as such, they are the biggest influences on who you become. They share a deep connection that not only supports the structure of your web, but the structure of your whole life. Perhaps it never occurred to you how fundamental they are to one another. Think about this for a minute.

Beliefs + Relationships + Experiences = YOU

- Your beliefs create your reality which forms your perception of your relationships and experiences.

Relationships + Beliefs = Experiences

- Your relationships and your beliefs create your life experiences.

Experiences + Relationships = Beliefs

- Your relationships and life experiences create your beliefs.

Beliefs + Experiences = Relationships

- Your beliefs and your experiences have the greatest impact on your relationships.

The truth is that before we hit adulthood, these three elements of our webs are already loaded with bugs. In discovering what's trapped within them you will *really* begin to understand yourself, and why things in your life bug you.

As beliefs, relationships and experiences are the core of you we will start to detangle your Web of Life through these elements. But before we dive into the web, I must show you a helpful trick that will prove useful on your path to complete self-understanding.

The Three Spheres

Imagine the three spheres as your starter kit to becoming an expert. This tool will uncover the mystery behind your web because it reveals the deeper truths within the elements. It's simple to use and easy to understand because it works just like the zoom function on your phone.

You know your web was not woven alone. You may be at its core, but you were raised within a family, a country and a planet. The three spheres gives you an authentic look at the wider impacts on your web and a more comprehensive understanding of the eight elements so you grasp how everything is ultimately connected.

The Self Sphere
Zooming into the smallest sphere shines the spotlight on you. You take centre stage surrounded only by the eight fundamentals. Looking through this lens focuses on your personal connection to each element.

So energy looks at your mental, emotional, physical and spiritual energy. Relationships begins with the one you have with yourself and includes your relationship to emotions like happiness, anger, fear and sadness. You look at your self beliefs and your personal beliefs about everyone and everything. Your environments are the physical places that you lived and interacted within, as well as your emotional and mental environment.

History in the self sphere is the story of your life, which means your childhood and all of your experiences. Science is your knowledge of the information available and how you apply it in your everyday life. For example, your awareness of the research behind the impacts of stress on the mind and body.

As you are the main character in your life, your natural instinct will be to look at your web through the self sphere alone. However this is the least practical and effective way to grasp a true understanding of your web and of yourself.

The Social Sphere
To uncover the main influences on your web, you need to zoom out of the self and into the social sphere. It's the sphere of your society - all the people and places that have impacted on your life. That includes your family, friends, the people in your local community, and extends out to your state and country. The institutions that played a role in your life are considered under this sphere too, such as government, education, religion, economics and healthcare.

If someone other than you comes to mind when you think about an element in your web, chances are they are part of your social sphere. For example, looking at beliefs through this lens considers the beliefs of those around you and how they've influenced your web. History through this perspective sees how the personal histories of your family members over multiple generations has affected your web and infiltrated your self sphere. But the truth is there are greater powers shaping the webs and spheres of everyone around you, which has bearings on your own.

The World Sphere
Zoomed all the way out, you are looking at your web (and anyone else's) through the lens of the world. This sphere begins by looking at the geographical region that you were born into and raised within, and includes the whole world. It takes a global approach to help you make sense of the way the elements played out in your life.

To comprehend what directly and indirectly shaped the webs of those in your social sphere, you'll likely need to know about major historical events that happened on the other side of the world. This perspective highlights the powerful influences that shaped the choices made by those around you. You may be surprised to discover just how deeply world events have impacted the people in your social sphere, which in turn affected the elements in your web.

To obtain the most accurate results you must look at your web from the world sphere in rather than the self sphere out. All of our webs have been impacted by the world in different ways over many generations. The simplest way to see this using the three spheres is through the beliefs and history strand. So let's take a brief look at this strand for a moment.

No element in the Web of Life has left a more monumental imprint on human history than beliefs. Belief systems have fuelled the division of the world, regions, continents, countries and states all the way down to friendships, families and partnerships. So to understand why you were raised with a specific belief system, you need to know world history as it relates to the country and region in which your family originated.

It is likely that your ancestors followed the predominant religion of their country and then passed that belief system onto future generations. Regardless of whether you forged your own path of faith in later life or followed what you were born into, the world sphere influence remains the same.

Many wars were waged throughout history based on religion. Groups or individuals believed theirs was right and that all others were wrong. Difference was unacceptable, so you had to conform for protection and survival, flee for safety, or you were killed. At times people were not even given the freedom to make a choice. This is the history of many countries, but isn't just woven into the webs of the Indigenous peoples. As it is the ugly history of my home country, Australia, it is embedded within the history element of everyone who calls themselves Australian.

STUFF THAT SHOULD STICK

🕸 There are 8 fundamental elements in your Web of Life.

🕸 The 3 spheres are a crucial tool to expand your self-awareness.

🕸 Each element is tied to its counterpart to form the 4 strands of your web.

🕸 **Beliefs + Relationships + Experiences = YOU**
(and these 3 elements are the core of your web).

🕸 Your beliefs create your reality which influences your perception of your relationships and experiences.

CHAPTER 2

Understanding Cycles

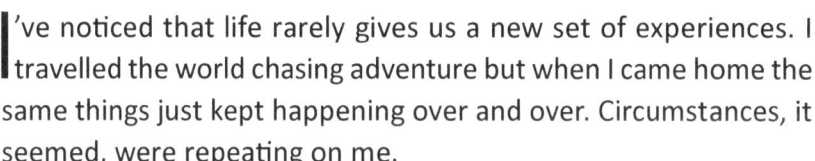

I've noticed that life rarely gives us a new set of experiences. I travelled the world chasing adventure but when I came home the same things just kept happening over and over. Circumstances, it seemed, were repeating on me.

It was different people, in different places and at different times, yet the experiences remained the same; betrayal, loss, deceit, conflict, stress and denial. It was a never-ending cycle that was impossible to escape. Unless I left the country! I wanted so badly for things to be different, but felt helpless to create lasting change in my life.

After doing some research into it I found that everything revolves in cycles. Our world functions within lunar, seasonal, agricultural, financial and menstrual cycles. Time runs in a cycle of days, weeks, months and years. Astrology is based on planetary cycles and their energetic influence on us.

Science has mapped the lifecycles of every single thing in existence; from carbon and rocks to stars and galaxies. Events repeat yearly: reunions, birthdays, tax, grand finals, religious holidays and festivals. It's even how we experience the mundane, from putting fuel in the car to paying bills, fees and subscriptions.

Cycles are so deeply ingrained in human life that we seem to forget they exist. If everything is on a constant loop, then why would my experiences be any different? The answer struck like lightning and then the epiphanies starting rolling in like thunder.

I saw my *whole* life as nothing but a bunch of cycles. Living room, bedroom. Sleep, wake up. Go to work, go home. Weekdays, weekends. And they were all smaller cycles inside of a bigger one. But it went far deeper than that. Everything happening inside of me, from my thoughts and feelings to everything happening outside of me - it's all anything was. A cycle. And then cycles within cycles.

Suddenly I was seeing them everywhere. Now when friends told me their problems, it's all I noticed. I was surprised at how often I was hearing it around me, yet it never registered before. I wondered who actually understood the weight of their words when they talked about a 'vicious cycle' in their lives. So let me ask you, do you find the same things keep happening to you? Are you repeatedly experiencing the same thoughts and emotions?

We all have perpetual cycles in our lives that we want to change and I've found some popular ones. Like repeatedly having the same argument with someone or going for the same type of people or personalities in new relationships. I realised I had a relationship cycle where I was always with the same character, just with different avatars.

Getting Bugged

One night whilst I sat on my balcony pondering cycles and the Web of Life, a few metres away in between two trees a massive spider was weaving one. It was so peaceful to watch it spiral around the web from the inside out and it looked beautiful, glistening in the moonlight. I was strangely jealous. There was *no way* my web looked anything like that, or anyone else's for that matter. But then again, spiders start over almost daily, whereas we're stuck with the same one for life.

So I started contemplating how it is that we weave our webs. It certainly isn't the calm and calculated choreography of a spider moving from strand to strand. Considering my experience at the time I thought, if I were a spider I would be frantically jumping all over the place and going around in circles.

I tried to imagine what my web would look like and just saw total chaos. But then I thought, how could it *not* be? Life was always interrupting and throwing curveballs that had me spiralling out of control. Life for a spider is so simple… just weave, eat and chill. There's no complication in that.

That's when it hit me. Bugs! Spider webs are built to catch bugs and insects so they can eat. The bugs in my web, however, were the obstacles in my life. The traumas and the problems that got in my way. They stopped me from weaving peacefully, and had me going around in circles. It had never occurred to me before, but I realised we actually have sayings about this. Think about the meaning behind the phrases, don't bug me, it's bugging me and bugger off.

My bug theory fit perfectly in the Web of Life, and like magic my thoughts returned to cycles and instantly it all made sense!

Cycles in Your Web

So we are either spiralling within or weaving around our webs. When your life is going smoothly, you weave around all the elements in your web with ease and flow, like a spider. These are positive cycles, and they don't cause you any dramas. A negative cycle, however, is when you are stuck spiralling around a bug that's caught somewhere in your web, and this results in a negative experience.

But where'd the bug come from? Well, the truth is that it all started *with* a negative experience. Ultimately it bugged you enough to get a bug stuck in your web. Then each time you spiralled around it afterwards you trapped it further and further in your web. Eventually your spiralling will completely surround it.

You see, some of these bugs were caught so long ago that now they look like cocoons. So you're left with a huge knot in your web that can be seen from space, and it weighs you down. These cocoon-looking knots in your web are your deepest and most powerful cycles, and they're always going to be the hardest to break.

In this book you'll discover how to recognise the bugs you keep spiralling around, which will empower you to take control of the cycles that seem to control you. Then I will reveal how you can break them for good. But before we get into any of this, first you need to know the kinds of cycles we have and how they are connected to one another.

Whether they are positive or negative, there are three types of cycles in your Web of Life.

Mental Cycles
We tend to live in our minds. Thoughts are constant and can be a nightmare to tame, which is why you may struggle with meditation like I do. But when your mind roams freely, all you find is the same thoughts popping up over and over again. These thinking loops in your mind are your mental cycles.

We have so much more going on inside than we would ever want to express. It's like the mind lives on overdrive! So we keep most of our inner world hidden and carefully select what we share with the outside world. To be fair, the stuff that keeps coming up isn't exactly the greatest.

Although these thoughts can be positive or negative, they are negative when they originated from or are connected to painful experiences. Whenever you think a thought you have completed a mental cycle. Every time you remember a past event you complete another cycle. Anytime you have a negative thought about yourself, there's another one. Thinking about someone else again? You catch my drift.

A negative mental cycle means you are spiralling around a bug. The more you feed a mental cycle with energy, the stronger it becomes and as a result, the more you experience an increase in its repetition. When this happens it means the cycle has linked up with an emotional one.

Emotional Cycles
You initially experience life through the lens of emotion, which guides your thoughts about the situation and determines how you see yourself in it. Your emotions don't just colour how you experience life though, but also how you interpret information and how you express yourself.

When you find an emotion keeps arising, that's an emotional cycle. Whether it happens purposely or not, you then start to think into what you feel. Your mental cycles are attached to emotional ones, just like your thoughts are connected to your feelings. One will always be tied to the other.

When a mental and an emotional cycle is fed energy and attention over time they bind together, gaining strength and momentum. From then on, whenever that thought or feeling surfaces, it will immediately reactivate the other half of the cycle. The longer this process continues the more powerful it becomes and when it finally reaches tipping point, it becomes physical.

A mental cycle + an emotional cycle = a physical cycle

Physical Cycles
When a mental and emotional cycle combine forces, it results in a physical cycle. This is the appearance or expression of what's gone on beneath the surface. Depending on the nature of the other cycles and the individual person they will manifest differently, but physical cycles will always be expressed in more than one way.

There are some that you may recognise, such as panic attacks, sleep issues, violence, criticism, overeating, undereating, recurring dreams or nightmares, self-harm and health problems. An addiction is a physical cycle as are obsessive-compulsive actions, such as nail biting or skin picking. However, in my experience I have found the most common evidence is found in our verbal expression. It's as simple as telling the same story over and over, yelling, gossiping, lying or denial.

As they tend to show on the outside they are usually seen as your biggest problems, however physical cycles are only the symptoms. You know that your actions are the result of what goes on inside you, but remembering this is *crucial* to you understanding yourself and the negative cycles in your web.

The Trifecta

It's frustrating when you experience unwanted thoughts, feelings and actions on repeat, but you don't know why you keep doing it or how to stop. Well, if you have ever read *The Brain That Changes Itself* by Dr. Norman Doidge you would know that neurons that fire together, wire together. Your cycles are the same and when the three types fuse together they make a trifecta. So whenever one starts running, the other two follow.

Take the physical cycle of a smoking addiction. I know how hard this one it is to break because I've struggled with it since I was in my teens. For decades I tried to stop using support tools and strategies. My longest success streak was five years, but I always went back. Why did I do that?

It's because this physical cycle is just the resulting action (symptom) of a series of much deeper mental and emotional ones. You see, it was those that *actually* needed my attention. It was more important to understand and break these cycles first, as they're the force behind the smoking. The addiction itself is just the physical symptom.

I'm not going to lie, addressing the inner ones was harder than quitting. It took a while to identify all the mental and emotional cycles tied to it, and learn how to recognise them in action. I discovered I had many beliefs attached to that act, including that it helped me think and solve problems. I don't know why any of this surprised me though; I'd been smoking since I was twelve.

In the process of cutting down, I became aware of their inner-workings. Uncovering the connections between my emotional cycles and my mental ones was where the *real* difficulty lay, and breaking those cycles was challenging. But, incredibly, breaking the physical cycle afterwards was effortless.

Cycles That Stick

I need you to know that some cycles have cascaded from the world sphere, through your social sphere and into the self sphere. These are generational. Although you didn't trap that particular bug in your web, you need to be the one to break the cycle and free it.

So it doesn't really matter if a cycle is inherited or self-created. Either way they will be perpetuated until you can identify the helpful from the hindering, and consciously break the negative ones so you can replace them with positive ones.

It's easy to stick to negative cycles because they are familiar to you and let's face it, you're more comfortable when things are familiar (even when it sucks). You know how to avoid conflict and confrontation if you have been doing it your whole life. That cycle needs no real effort from you to continue. A new one where you stand up for yourself and speak your truth, however, is a different story. This is why it will always be easier to stick with old cycles, no matter how problematic they are.

Understanding Cycles

Uncovering your own is the first step to detangling your Web of Life. In this book I will be sharing some of the most common ones we get stuck in and you'll learn how to observe your trifectas in action. To be able to break a cycle you must understand how it was made in the first place. So now that you understand all the basics of cycles I can reveal how they are created.

The 4mation of a Cycle

You have an **experience** in life. You learn information from it that you consider as **knowledge**. **Integration** is when you process and embody this knowledge and then it comes out in your **expression**. These are the stages of a cycle's 4mation.

Experiences are the best part of being alive and being human, though some can be scarring. Either way you learn information from every experience. This becomes the knowledge you use to start a cycle. Integration occurs as you mentally process this information, which instantly binds to the emotions you felt at the time.

This is where a mental cycle connects with an emotional one. How you process the knowledge determines whether it's positive, negative or neutral and it's mostly influenced by your emotions. As this knowledge is integrated a belief is formed, which may be specific to the situation, certain individuals involved, yourself or all of the above. All that's left to do is bring the inside out, and that's where expression comes in.

This might be you telling the story of your experience, but physical cycles always manifest in more than one way. Just think of all the things you'll say and do when someone or something bugs you. So once these stages have come full circle and it's become physical, a trifecta is created and the cycle's 4mation is complete.

Whether it sticks depends on how much mental, emotional and physical energy you proceed to feed it. Anytime you repeat the cycle after its 4mation you spiral around that bug and trap it further in your web. The reason they stick so easily is because as soon as an inner part starts the rest of the cycle will follow, which happens so quickly and so often you're usually unaware of it.

All it takes is one experience to start a cycle, and it doesn't even have to be your own. They can also begin with someone sharing a negative experience with you. Regardless if it was first-hand or not, as you process the information a fear is created inside you. Then from that moment on, that experience is seen as a guaranteed outcome in that situation, not just one of many possibilities.

Relationships are a great example. We all know being cheated on is a defining moment and an emotionally damaging experience.

Perhaps this is something you know all too well. Either way, let me ask you. What are the chances you can forgive without holding onto the fear it'll happen again? Or going into the next relationship without being fearful you'll be cheated on?

Slim to none, right? You can't help it when that four-letter 'f' word is involved. It doesn't matter how much you want to believe your partner's faithful or how honest they are with you, the fear just takes over. It consumes your thoughts and stops your heart from being open so you can't be hurt again. It's that easy to turn your knowledge of one bad experience into an expectation for all others in the future.

You see, your emotions direct your thoughts. You may be under the illusion that cycles start in the mind, but they don't. They start in the body. Your body may be bugged when something happens to you, but it's your mind that starts running rings around it and doesn't let it go. It believes it's in your best interests to take that experience and create a cycle with it. This is because fear creates beliefs with incredible speed and power.

You're not necessarily aware you've integrated your knowledge this way, but cycles that are fear-based shift your perception of the event and make you believe it *will* happen again rather than it *might*. Fear presents information to the mind as factual so this belief quickly gets expressed through both actions and inactions, all in the name of self-protection. Fear can be so debilitating you withdraw or shutdown completely but at the same time so motivating that you behave in ways that are totally out of character.

So now we can start exploring each of the eight fundamental elements in your Web of Life and uncover some of the most common cycles we get stuck in.

STUFF THAT SHOULD STICK

🕸 Everything revolves in cycles and our whole world revolves around and functions within them.

🕸 You're stuck in a negative cycle when you spiral around a bug caught in your web.

🕸 We have 3 types of cycles: mental, emotional and physical

🕸 **A mental cycle + an emotional cycle = a physical cycle**

🕸 The secret to breaking a physical cycle is to uncover the connection between the emotional and mental ones.

🕸 **Experience + Knowledge + Integration + Expression = the 4mation of a cycle**

🕸 An **experience** gives you **knowledge** which you **integrate** before it's **expressed**, which means a cycle has formed.

CHAPTER 3

Element 1: Beliefs

Your beliefs determine how you see everything - the world, yourself, the people around you and events that occur. They shape your perception of life, thus creating your reality. However most of your beliefs are unconscious, so they sit just beneath your awareness where they're never really understood enough to actually be reflected upon. Yet whenever they're challenged you will instinctively fight for their survival.

As they're at the core of all your thoughts, feelings and actions, this element is not only fundamental to your web, but to every cycle you have now or will ever create in the future. The truth is that none of the ideas behind them were your own to begin with. You were introduced to them all. From birth, your beliefs were influenced by those in your social sphere. You were directed into certain ways of thinking and feeling through your exposure to places, people and their ideas.

In Chapter 1 you learned that **Relationships + Experiences = Beliefs**. Relationships are your main source of information and experiences in life, both of which guide your beliefs and create your cycles. So as these fundamental elements are the foundation of your web, your beliefs will always be tied to these two elements too.

So why start with beliefs? Well, this strand is connected to its counterpart - history. These elements are forever tied together, so to reflect on your beliefs is to reflect upon your history. To discover the origins of your beliefs you must first look at your relationship history and your experiences. This is where we begin to detangle your web, uncover your biggest knots, and reveal the core experiences (bugs) underneath the cycles that stop you from living your best life!

Element 1: Beliefs

Belief Cycles

Your core beliefs continually replay in your mind, so if you can't move forward in life it's these that are holding you back. Although you have 100% control over your beliefs, you first have to be aware of what you believe in order to discern the helpful from the hindering. For many of us, making our unconscious beliefs conscious will be the hardest part of identifying our cycles.

There are more bugs stuck in this element than I can write about in one chapter (even an entire book). But I can tell you that self beliefs are a major knot in all our webs. Believing you are not good enough is commonly formed by the cycle of unworthiness. Though this problem appears to be mental, it's the strong emotions that give this belief all its power and forces the cycle to become physical.

The emotional cycle makes you feel unworthy, perhaps of love, success, praise or happiness. This triggers the mental cycle, so you think that you don't deserve these things. But you don't just believe you're not good enough for them, you act on it physically which strengthens the cycle in your web and ensures you repeat it again!

The first step to detangling your web is to figure out the core experience that created this cycle. This might bring up painful memories, but it shows you that the idea wasn't yours to begin with. The belief was formed by another person's perception of you, which came from an experience in your childhood. But it's not always the people in your social sphere that you'd expect, like your family or friends. For many of us it was actually a teacher.

When someone said something negative about you it made you feel like you weren't good enough. The detailed information presented at the time was enough evidence to prove this idea to be true, so you integrated this knowledge and boom - now this idea has become a fact! The belief that you are unworthy is not just a thought and an emotion, but also a fear that lives inside you.

A negative belief won't be overturned simply by hearing opposition. So after it was created, anything positive you were told about yourself wasn't integrated as it didn't align with the cycle of unworthiness. Your belief was not "I am amazing", so comments to that effect weren't considered factual. Only information that supported this belief was gathered from your experiences, which in turn strengthened the cycle. Eventually you spiralled so much internally that the cycle had to *physically* come out of you.

Though they are complete cycles themselves, perfectionism and productivity are the two most popular expressions of this cycle. It's important to note that both of these likely co-exist within you, you just might be unaware of the fact that they're rooted in a lack of self-worth.

The Cycle of Perfectionism
When you believe you're not good enough, nothing you ever do or say is acceptable (for you or anyone else). So you might try to look and act perfect at all times so you feel like you are worthy. If everything you do is perfect, then you must be too, right? It's easy to see this cycle is never-ending because nothing or no one is. This is why striving for perfection is a losing battle - you will forever fall short.

This means no amount of effort or improvement is seen as a win because you already believe you're less than. Yet you can't stop trying to make everything perfect; from your appearance to your work to the presentation of your home. You spend countless hours feeding energy to this cycle, which perpetuates it in your life and then through your expectations you inflict it onto those around you.

Element 1: Beliefs

The Cycle of Productivity

If you still aren't good enough when you're doing your best, then maybe you will be if you do as much as possible. You might try to be highly productive so you feel like you've accomplished enough to make you worthy of good things. This cycle is deeply rooted in childhood environments because you were usually measured based on how productive and effective you were around the house and at school. But your work is never done because it's never quite enough.

Then naturally, this cycle is enforced in the work environment. Often the most valuable employee is the one who does the most. The focus on performance and productivity keeps this cycle repeating well into adulthood. You believe you need to keep doing things to prove to those around you that you are valuable or else you feel lazy and worthless. No wonder we are so exhausted that we prefer to order Uber Eats for dinner and binge Netflix all night. But how guilty do you feel afterwards for not doing stuff around the house?

The Cycle of Appearances

This particular cycle is based on the idea that nothing is good enough, and it starts being inflicted on us by our family. As children many of us learnt that our parents cared more about how everything appeared to others than anything else, including how we felt. Therefore you were taught that what other people think is more important than the truth. So the message was clear - how things look on the outside matters the most.

This is the most common belief cycle in history and it's been revolving for generations. You repeat this cycle whenever you are fearful of how something looks and you do this because deep down you think you're not good enough. Now you will have beliefs about how you and your life looks to you, but the cycle becomes physical when you filter what others can see in an effort to influence what they believe. You do this so you can save face when you don't think the truth will make you look good.

We all have positivity and negativity in our lives and in ourselves, but both sides are never shown equally. To be raw with others takes courage because being open, honest and authentic leaves you exposed and vulnerable. You fear people's judgement and negative perceptions so you won't let them see the truth. Instead, you reflect only what you want them to know and what you think makes you come off best.

You usually put on a front to conceal your reality because you don't want to face it. How much do you let people see how it *really* is? Your house is a mess but you shove everything in cupboards or under furniture immediately before guests arrive. Your personal life is in pieces, but you pretend you've got it all figured out. You're drowning in a sea of paperwork but say you've got it under control. Your relationship is falling apart but you tell everyone it's fine.

You also see this cycle functioning in governments, corporations and workplaces all over the world. You see it in families, friends, marriages and partnerships. We do it to ourselves and we do it to each other. This cycle operates across all three spheres and exists within everyone's Web of Life.

Breaking this one will make you a generational cycle breaker and you will likely be the first person in your family to even attempt it. But first you must admit you're perpetuating this cycle and learn to recognise when you're doing it. Unfortunately we repeat it so often it can be hard to recognise this cycle in action.

The mental cycle is thinking 'I can't tell the truth' because the emotional cycle is feeling shame or embarrassment about it.

Element 1: Beliefs

What goes on inside pushes to be expressed outside, so if it ain't pretty on the inside then it's going to come out ugly too. The physical cycles used to influence the perception of others vary, but typically centre around verbal expressions. Some of these are denial, falsehood, fake identity, storytelling and my personal go-to - the cycle of deflection.

When a conversation is moving towards talking about my life and it isn't positive, I will deflect by asking the person follow up questions about their situation to get back on the subject of them. I could spend hours catching up with a friend and we leave each other without them knowing a single thing that's happening in my life. It's a completely different story when things are going great, though.

I'm not avoiding discussion about my life so I don't bring the other person down... it's *all* about self-preservation. It's my ego behind the wheel! How I feel about my reality stops me from sharing any information with others because if I can't face it alone, I certainly don't want to face it in the presence of another person. If I won't tell it like it is, I won't tell it at all.

No matter what cycle is used to avoid being open about how it really is, the fact remains that the truth is being dodged, and it's not just in the company of others. The ego doesn't know how to handle it, and doesn't want to. So we tell elaborate stories instead of the truth. We deny the existence of the issue at all. We tell the lies that we want to believe. We act like everything's great. There may be a select few people we are honest and raw with, but for the most part we keep the real inside and push out the fake. We all repeat this cycle on some level!

Identifying Negative Belief Cycles

We all perpetuate these cycles I've shared with you to varying degrees. You might notice them in those around you, but it's only a mirror reflecting back what's inside you. To truly understand yourself you must be able to acknowledge the cycles in your own web. Then you can start to become aware of exactly *how* you spiral around that bug and recognise *when* you're doing it.

Knowing the why of belief cycles is often straightforward. In most cases, it didn't start with you. To break the cycles in the beliefs element of your web, you first have to distinguish between what's been passed down from others (inflicted) and what's come from the knowledge you took from your own experiences. You'd be surprised how often and how easily we confuse the two.

Tim was a man in his mid-twenties with cancer who was only comfortable being angry. As he shared his life story with me I was moved to tears. There was so much pain and heartache. When I told him I was sorry and that I wanted to help him he quickly retorted that I didn't really care about him because no one did.

At first I was shocked by his comment, but then he shared the core experience that instilled this belief in him and suddenly it all made sense. Not only did it clarify why I never saw him upset, but it explained why he was so angry all the time. Since he was three years old, whenever he cried his father told him to stop because 'no one cares'. This continued for a decade until he left home, preferring the streets.

See how easily a negative belief gets inflicted? One of the biggest problems with cycles is that they get repeated unconsciously, and the same goes for our beliefs. Tim was unaware that his belief was inflicted and that hearing it repeatedly didn't make it a fact. I couldn't argue with him about it because his mind was made up; it turned out many other people had told him they cared but had always let him down.

So I'm not kidding when I tell you that your limiting beliefs aren't even yours! You must become aware of exactly what it is that you believe, what experience is behind it, who gave you the idea and how much energy you're still feeding it. To know the *real* you, you need to peel back the layers put on you by those in your social sphere. Only then can you discover who *you* really are, liberated from the negative beliefs that have been inflicted on you.

Breaking these cycles begins with acceptance and awareness. So now that you are aware of some belief cycles, start to recognise those that you repeat. Once you are conscious of a cycle's existence you can learn exactly how it unfolds and accept that breaking it is your responsibility.

There's a belief inside everything you say and do, then there's a core experience behind it. But it's the belief that's pushing you to perpetuate the cycle, and it's only when you are aware of it that you can decide which ones serve you and which ones don't. So after you have identified a negative belief, the next step is to identify the core experience that began the 4mation of the cycle.

Even if you can't pinpoint the exact situation that started it, you will always find that you were introduced to the ideas in your belief by someone else. There are many cycles in this element that stop you from weaving around your web with ease and flow, but you must start detangling yours so you can decide which beliefs you need to keep and which ones you need to let go of.

"Beliefs have the power to create and the power to destroy. Human beings have the awesome ability to take any experience of their lives and create meaning that disempowers them or one that can literally save their lives."

- Tony Robbins

STUFF THAT SHOULD STICK

- Beliefs shape our perception of life, thereby creating our reality.

- **Beliefs = Experiences + Relationships**

- The 4 most common belief cycles are unworthiness, perfection, productivity and appearances, which we all repeat on some level.

- Whether they are positive, negative or neutral, most of your beliefs were inflicted upon you by those in your social sphere.

- After you recognise a negative or limiting belief, revealing the experience at its core will unveil the 4mation of the cycle and allow you to decide if you want to continue it or break it.

CHAPTER 4

Element 2: Relationships

This element is fundamental to your Web of Life because human connection is vital to your growth and development. We are social beings that are innately wired to seek relationships, which makes sense since without them we wouldn't have survived long after birth. The bonds you share with people are critical to your mental and emotional well-being, but are also essential for learning - about yourself, others and the world around you.

Our relationships are the source of our greatest joys and pleasures in life, yet they are the source of our deepest pains, frustrations and traumas too. Since none of us came with a manual about how to navigate our complex selves it's understandable that we face challenges when connecting with other complicated beings.

The art of relationships is difficult to master and we all go into them with needs and expectations that remain unmet. So we are left with disappointment and resentment gradually builds over time. This could be for the positive experiences that never happened, but it's usually more about the negative ones that actually did.

As you know, all it takes is one bad experience to start a cycle, which means that one bad experience in a relationship has the power to affect all others. How does this happen? During the 4mation of a cycle a belief is created based on the knowledge you gained from an experience, which changes how you behave in relationships. Remember that **Relationships + Experiences = Beliefs**.

People Power

Your life happens alongside your relationships and the good times bond you with people and form great memories. The not so good ones can create a series of dangerous cycles that are detrimental to your health at best and at worst, deadly. One devastating experience can completely alter your perception of people and of relationships. Afterwards you cannot go back to how you saw and felt, or who you once were. This is particularly true for those of us who have gone through significant traumas early on in life, but we will get to that when we explore the Childhood element.

Negative experiences within any relationship may cause you to disconnect from that one person, although it is just as easy to disconnect from people in general and create negative beliefs that impact your future relationships. When you've been hurt a shift can take place in a heartbeat and doors that used to be open are slammed shut.

One experience can leave a lifelong mark and then you form limiting beliefs that are hard to shake. You relied on someone who let you down, so now you only depend on yourself. A person you loved betrayed you, so you don't let anyone in. Someone took advantage, so now you don't give anymore. You trusted the wrong person, so you've stopped trusting everyone.

Your experiences change your perspective of relationships and it's not always for the better. This tends to happen after someone breaks one of the pillars that relationships depend on like trust, acceptance, communication or respect. The pain resides in you as a fear of being vulnerable and has you living in survival mode. You remain hyper-vigilant and on high alert, finding red flags even when there are none. It clouds your judgement and affects your behaviour in other relationships.

Don't forget the possibility that this isn't the case for you, but is for someone you share a significant relationship with. We notice when others are closed off but don't try to understand why. This is the power people have. Reflect on those in your social sphere and consider how this may explain their impact on you. Though this is your Web of Life, you should always look outside of the self sphere first.

Relationship Cycles

We each have all different kinds of relationships, and across those there are many different cycles that can exist. To explore the cycles we usually get stuck in here it's best to look at those that repeat across all of them. Conflict is always one of the first things to come to mind and with good reason. It's likely to be your biggest challenge and causes you the most pain and suffering.

The truth is, it is irrelevant whether conflict remains purely internal or is frequently experienced externally. You suffer when you bottle everything up and when you let everything out. Who can honestly say they have healthy disagreements with others and resolve them calmly and rationally? Though conflict is a natural part of relationships, it is rare for people to have positive conflict cycles. To uncover the inner-workings of your own, you first need to understand where your methods of initiation and engagement originated.

> *"The family is one of the most powerful forces in nature. Family life is full of wonder, beauty and drama."*
>
> *- David Attenborough*

As children we learned from watching our close relationships, so you were introduced to conflict at home as a child. Depending on how family life was for you growing up, this could have been

Element 2: Relationships

through parents, siblings, grandparents, extended family members or family friends. For some of you it was through foster families.

Ideally, you had role models who showed you how a healthy and happy relationship functions. You saw people disagree respectfully, with each person expressing their thoughts and feelings in a supportive and understanding environment before coming to a fair resolution. Sadly, this was not what was modelled for the majority of us. No one intended to inflict their cycles onto you, but "monkey see, monkey do" is a well-known saying for this reason.

No cycle is ever guaranteed to be continued by you. However, your exposure to conflict influenced your perception of relationships as you were still developing your understanding of them. Long before you formed cycles of your own you watched dramas unfolding around you. So you saw how others engaged in or initiated conflicts.

The frequency with which you experienced certain behaviours in a disagreement increased the likelihood that you would behave in the same manner, or at the very least accept those same behaviours from others. If you unconsciously respond or react to your first serious conflict, it is quite natural to repeat exactly what you've seen at home. This is because your knowledge of the styles and strategies your family members used were integrated. So this will inevitably be expressed in the 4mation of your own cycle.

This means you started shaping your beliefs about what conflict looks, feels and sounds like based on what you learned watching those around you. Perhaps you believed you must scream the house down in order to be heard in an argument, or that expressing yourself causes problems, so you avoided it like the plague. Some people grew up believing that only violence ends conflicts whilst for others walking out was the only way to shut it down.

None of these are healthy responses to conflict, but when it's all you have ever known it is easy to fall into the cycles set before you, especially when they're generational. It takes a considerable effort to create positive conflict cycles in your life when it has never been part of your experience in relationships.

While I was separated I decided to figure out of the mechanics of my own conflict cycle and discovered my personal style was to withhold affection and say sarcastic comments. That was my way of showing that I had an issue but when I was approached with someone else's I would get extremely defensive and then give them the silent treatment afterwards. As difficult as it was to uncover how I expressed this cycle it was the key to transforming it completely.

I was then able to recognise I was repeating the physical part right in the midst of arguments. I was surprised to find that my expression was always the same, irrespective of who the conflict was with. But this allowed me to see that the other parts of the trifecta always operated the same way too. My emotional and mental cycles would always start spiralling long before the argument would occur, and it was what I did at this point that would force the conflict out.

The cycle only became physical once I had shared what was inside of me. But I would never go straight to the person the issue was with at first and I know I am not alone here. How often do you talk about your problems with someone other than who is involved? When you have an issue in a relationship, you don't discuss each time it arises with them or escalate every tiny matter into a conflict. You let it build up, right?

It's not good, but it's what we do! It's only after you have been spiralling internally for a while that you reach the point where expression is needed. This may have been going on for days or weeks before you're on the edge of conflict. When mental and emotional cycles have been revolving repeatedly the trifecta usually comes out verbally first. You might vent your frustration with a friend or colleague, allowing you to unleash some of that inner turmoil.

The problem is once your cycle has started to be expressed, the chances of something small triggering an emotional eruption or mental outburst significantly increase. An explosion will appear to come out of the blue because the person on the other end of it will have no idea what's been going on inside you. Yet you've been spiralling around that bug in your web for so long that now the fangs are out and an attack is imminent.

You see, many relationships are stuck in a conflict cycle. You believe the problem is the repeated arguments, which tend to be about the same or similar issues. This keeps causing you both pain and frustration as there is frequent tension and strain on the relationship. But the fighting is not the *real* problem. It is just the physical cycle you are both perpetuating.

I've honestly found that relationships suffer more due to the way disagreements are handled rather than the issue itself. Both of you end up being hurt by things that were said and done in the heat of the moment, and cannot move forward because nothing was resolved. So it happens again. And again. And again.

Soon your relationship becomes like a romantic drama series on Netflix which features a big blow up between the couple every single episode. Sure you have short bursts of peace and joy throughout each season, but you both know the inevitable fight scene is coming up. *Who will launch the first mouth missile in the next episode of 'Never Ending Argument'?*

When two people are stuck in this kind of relationship cycle, it seems impossible to break. You are both dying for it to stop and keep promising each other it will, but neither of you understand what *actually* needs to change. No wonder in less than a week you're back at each other's throats!

The expression of the cycle is what happens in a conflict, it's the part that you experience. Voices being raised, things being thrown, someone storming out, acting out, someone shutting down, blame and finger pointing, name-calling, swearing, speaking over each other, not speaking to each other. When the forms of anyone's expression are negative in the conflict cycle, it's harsh, hurtful and hinders the relationship.

But this is the only part of the trifecta that can be seen. The other two are hidden which makes the physical part look like the problem. This is the power of knowledge and integration, which is where your mental and emotional cycles are formed.

The mystery isn't the physical part of the cycle because what you say and do is obvious to anyone present. The mental and emotional cycles are the ones driving the conflict but they work behind the scenes. This is why relationships struggle to stop the fighting - wanting to change the result is pointless when you're ignoring the path that got you there.

You both must detangle your mental and emotional cycles *first* because they hide underneath your actions (or inactions) and push them into expression. Discovering your core beliefs about relationships will bring these hidden cycles to light. Breaking the physical part afterwards will be one hundred times easier when the force behind your expression is well-known and deeply understood.

Element 2: Relationships

Some cycles that exist in our relationships are difficult to break because both people aren't on the same page. At times it may appear as though you're looking at totally different books. The saying it takes two to tango shows that a conflict cycle requires the participation of both people. So if you gotta dance, wouldn't you rather mix it up and start to salsa instead?

If you have a conflict cycle in any of your relationships, it's not impossible to break it alone. It's just tricky. Preferably you want the other person working on understanding themselves too, so you have the best chance of creating a new and positive cycle together. The key to breaking this cycle is knowing *how* you both get to the point where you initiate or engage in conflict, not so much *why* you do it. But once you know your hows you can better communicate your whys to each other.

Have you noticed that while you're getting to know people you both share the positive sides of yourselves as much as possible? Over time however, the true selves come out of the shadows. This is where the relationship starts to form their own cycles, and both people's pre-existing ones begin to merge. However the 4mation of a conflict cycle can get quite ugly in some relationships.

Leah's relationship was a whirlwind of romance. She was showered with nothing but love, affection and gifts for more than a year. So naturally, she thought he was the perfect partner to spend her life with. What she had experienced created positive beliefs about the relationship and she believed she was living every woman's dream. It wasn't until her wedding day that she met the real him and the nightmare began.

After the ceremony when they were alone in the car he held the marriage certificate up to her face and said "I fucking own you, bitch". Before she could register her shock he started laying into her and didn't stop till they reached the reception. She spent years wanting to break the cycle of abuse in her marriage but didn't know how to. Anything she ever said or did would cause an argument and his only form of expression was violence.

It took him beating the life out of the twins in her stomach for her to understand that the only way to break it was to leave the marriage. Though Leah always regretted staying in the relationship as it resulted in twin pregnancy loss, hindsight gave her the knowledge that without that traumatic experience she was unlikely to come out alive.

When you fear the negative cycles in your relationship you're not realising your power over them. If you don't act, the cycle will inevitably continue and it doesn't matter how much you want things to change. But relationships also put you in situations where you must experience the negative cycles of others. You might feel helpless and think you are powerless, but those fears will physically hold you back and stop you from taking necessary action.

The beauty of relationships is that they allow you to run the gauntlet of life with others. So you are always given the chance to express your thoughts, feelings and actions. In doing so, what is deep inside of you, wounds and all are able to be seen, felt, heard and experienced by you and everyone around you. Since it's not always magic and sunshine coming out of us all, I call it infliction instead of projection. And we inflict on far more than just people.

If you have ever thrown or kicked something out of frustration because it didn't do what you wanted you will know exactly what I mean. The best part though is that through the mirror of another human being, everything inside of us comes out and is then able to be brought to our attention. When this happens we are given an opportunity to figure out the core experience (bug) so we can start to break the cycles attached to them. The problem is that our cycles in conflict are mostly negative, so expression occurs with minimal compassion and maximum indifference.

Some cold, hard truths will often come out in the midst of an argument. But as you are both in attack mode at the time, rather than connect with the truth of what you are shown or told about yourself in the heat of the moment, you instinctively go into defence mode. This may be expressed through avoidance of some kind (such as denial) but can also be through a counter-attack. This stops you from registering the information that was brought to your attention.

As you develop awareness of your own conflict cycles, you will learn how to share authentic truths with effective communication and accept the difficult ones. This way what you say and what you're told has a fighting chance of being heard, understood and addressed. I know it hurts to face the truth, even more so when you're told it in a hurtful way. You will feel like it's happening *to* you, but it's actually happening *for* you.

Every conflict in a relationship presents you with a chance to identify your bugs and detangle the knots so you are free to weave your Web of Life with ease and flow. You have to know and understand your inner cycles in order to do something about them. Only then can you experience the positive transformation you desire in your life.

STUFF THAT SHOULD STICK

- A belief is created in the integration phase of a cycle's 4mation based on the knowledge you gained from an experience. This is expressed in your behaviour in relationships with others.

- Your beliefs about conflict came from your exposure to the relationship cycles of those in your social sphere.

- To understand the inner-workings of your own conflict cycle you need to work backwards - after you identify the physical part focus your awareness on recognising the mental and emotional parts that come before your physical expression.

- Once you know *how* you engage in and initiate conflict, you will be able to notice when you're starting to repeat the cycle.

CHAPTER 5

Element 3: Experiences

This element represents everything that has and will ever happen to you. Each moment you're alive is an experience; some are good, some are bad and everything in between is neutral. Yet their sum total has moulded you into who you are now and this element will forever be the most fundamental influence on the person you become.

There are infinite ways to view an experience as all of our perspectives are both unique and individual. Your perception is shaped by your life experiences, which are physical, mental, emotional and spiritual in nature. This is the crucial point from which your cycles begin and here lies the origin of the kinds of cycles we have.

The Super Strand

Of all life's stages, none of them impacts us quite like childhood. No wounds stay as raw and no scars run as deep as those made during this significant time period. The childhood element is tied to experiences to make this strand of your Web of Life.

How you see everything to how you think and feel about yourself, other people, the world around you and each aspect of life is determined by this strand. It's the ultimate creator of perception, which is why I call it the super strand.

The super strand is always jam-packed full of bugs you've caught from core moments in your journey. Think about it - *every* bug in *every* element in your Web of Life was first an experience, and many of the major ones occurred during childhood!

We spend our whole lives trying to make sense of ourselves based on the painful and difficult experiences of our pasts, and it always goes back to childhood. Many of us are plagued by our earliest sufferings because we don't know how to cope with the imprints they left behind. You may still find yourself dealing with consequences in their aftermath.

The thoughts and emotions attached to those memories are embedded so deeply within that they can be hard to let go of. They're such a huge part of who you are. Though there is some truth to this, I've learned there's a big difference between defining their impact on you and defining yourself *by* them.

I was in my late twenties when I became aware that I had been making this mistake and was shocked to discover that I had no clue who I actually was. It's one thing for pain to be part of your personal story, but another thing entirely to form your person and your story around your pain. If you're anything like me, it took a long time to realise that you are *not* what happened to you, you were simply the *experiencer*... and every soul must experience!

The Nature of Experience

How quickly and easily do you get lost in your experiences? No matter where you are or what you're doing they have the power to take you back into the past or project you into the future. You could say we are all seasoned time-travellers who are capable of imagining lengthy and detailed scenarios that never happened and never will. While reading this book I am sure that something will make you time-travel to the past, and probably more than once.

What dimension are *you in* during those memory periods? What dimension do those imagined possibilities exist in? I can hardly call them moments because after you return to the now you have no clue how much time has passed. Regardless of how long you were gone for you may find yourself leaving again in an instant. Hours of your day can go by where you've barely spent more than a few minutes fully immersed in the moment.

Speaking of time, what period would you consider yourself in when these shifts occur? Though you remain present physically, mentally and emotionally you're back in the past or off in some imagined future. You see, time really *is* an illusion because experience is multi-dimensional by nature!

So how often do you disconnect from a present experience to relive a past one? This always happens to me when I'm driving and it's only once I arrive at my destination that it hits me - I didn't spend a second enjoying the drive, which is ironic since I opted for the scenic route! I also realise I didn't have a clue what was happening around me the entire time.

I call it the rearview cycle because you keep looking back at what is behind you. This is a common experience cycle which is why people like Eckhart Tolle try to help us break it. However, we also go forward into the future just as much when we're stuck in the cycle of doom. This is where you keep envisioning fear-based possibilities and frequently imagine all kinds of things going wrong down the track.

Now you may believe this is purely a mental and emotional experience, however your body has a physical reaction to it. While you're playing out a scenario that hasn't happened (and likely never will) your body is overtaken by anxiety and fear. All this unfolds over your present experience, even though it's just an imagined future only happening inside your mind and body.

Element 3: Experiences

This is because experiences occur *within* experiences. Think about it. Being present in the moment is an experience and so is not being present. But you still experience your thoughts and emotions whether you're in the moment or not. Reliving a past event is an experience and imagining a future one is too.

Keep in mind that thinking about what happened yesterday or 5 minutes ago is the past and thinking about tomorrow or 5 minutes from now is the future. We jump in and out of the past, present and future constantly. Experience certainly *is* multi-dimensional when all of this can transpire simultaneously in under a minute!

You only go through an experience once, but thanks to your memories you can spend decades going back over it. Again and again. Memories can keep popping up a long time after the fact. So whenever our brain makes a connection to the past we will start to tap in and out of the present moment, which for the most part is out of our control!

A negative comment from someone takes you back to the criticism you copped as a kid. Someone's actions trigger the memory of when you were hurt by similar behaviours. A friend shares the story of their past pain, next minute you start silently rehashing your own. No matter which way it goes down, one thing remains the same - you are immediately transported out of the moment.

You may not have seen it this way before, but these are mental cycles. They don't occur in isolation though, as an emotional one always runs alongside it. The memories that resurface and the visualisations in your mind cause strong and powerful emotions to arise within your body. The physical sensations you feel trick your mind into believing it is actually happening now, and projecting yourself forward in time has the exact same effect.

Perspective is Everything

> *"Emotion conditions the mind and leads it to adopt a certain perspective, a certain view of things."*
>
> - Matthieu Ricard, *The Art of Meditation*

Anything has the power to unlock your greatest transformation. It can be as simple as watching a documentary, a movie, reading a book or having a meaningful conversation with a stranger. It can be as complicated as depression, divorce or the death of a loved one. Even an indirect experience can change your perspective, like hearing someone's story or seeing someone's strength through hardship.

As you weave your web you are shaping your views on all aspects of life. So no matter how minor things seem, anything can be life-altering because the repercussion of experience is *perspective*. Once your perspective shifts it changes your attitude and your energy, which impacts how you approach all future experiences.

You see, how you feel and what you think depends on your perspective. It directs the way you interpret the information you receive. Your mental and emotional processing also creates physical sensations you feel in your body. When we experience this energetic shift it can trigger a reactive outburst so we can expel that energy felt inside of us.

How we perceive what we experience is based on our emotions and so is how we react to our experiences. This explains why we confuse emotions with who and what we are rather than seeing them as they are; just another part of life that we experience. So no one is an angry or fearful person, they just perceive through the lens of anger or fear and react from that emotion too.

Element 3: Experiences

We truly underestimate the power our experiences have over us. They force us to think and feel which makes us react or respond on impulse. We do this with maximum speed and minimal forethought, so we don't digest the abundance of information our senses have picked up on. Without the time needed to clarify and question how we've interpreted this data overload, we don't know what our inner cycles are. So we just react as a knee-jerk response inspired by our perception, another part of our experience we rarely question.

We keep forgetting that experience is subjective, so no two people ever perceive things exactly the same. Even when you've shared an experience alongside another person, you might've gone through it together, but you will both see it in your own way. Each of you views and processes what's happened based on your own perspectives. That's why we call it a personal experience!

Do you think everyone who reads this book will view it the same way you do? Of course not. How each individual sees, understands, interprets and applies this content will be as unique to them as their web is to yours. How everyone connects with the information will also be deeply personal. How we go into an experience and how we come out of it also works the same way, it really is each to their own.

The way you perceive everything and everyone you come across is directly related to *your* life experiences. As a result, when you judge another person you automatically make two huge mistakes. First, you're looking at their life and reflecting upon how *you* would've done things, without having lived their specific series of experiences. Second, you're doing this from the perspective of someone who has woven a totally different web.

Even if you have life events in common, your personal experiences have completely original factors, not to mention the fact that they've been combined with other experiences. So you will always be coming from the perspective of your own Web of Life, which is based solely off of your own experiences. Both of which, is unlike theirs. So how can we possibly judge?

It can be really difficult to get why people make the choices they do, particularly without ever having lived their life. But it is *their* web! It made them who they are, led them down the paths they took and taught them all the lessons they've learned. Yet rather than understanding this, we judge from inside our own webs whilst neglecting to even factor that in in the first place.

You instinctively believe that if their web had've been your own you wouldn't have made the same decisions they did. Maybe you wouldn't have. Automatically you assume that you would have been capable of handling it all without following in any of their footsteps. Let's just say you didn't. The entire time you're foolishly thinking that you would've ended up the exact same person that you are now. No way in hell! Who's to say you would have even survived their life at all?

Only if you deeply consider the eight fundamental elements in their Web of Life can you have the slightest chance of being able to put yourself in their shoes to understand them and appreciate their perspective. It is my hope that from now on rather than judging someone, you will use the Web of Life to *get* them, and yourself, *completely*.

The Power of a Single Experience

Life lessons come in all shapes, sizes and situations. So every experience can impact you and in several ways. What you discover

Element 3: Experiences

(if anything) and how you change (if at all) depends on you, but one major event has the potential to transform you forever.

Experiences hit people differently, so how each person copes and how they are affected will vary. After going through the very same thing one person could be motivated, empowered and inspired to evolve whereas another could be paralysed, defeated and broken into a million pieces. I'm sure you know someone who became fearful, depressed or hateful because of something that happened. (Maybe that someone is you.)

Monumental experiences can have lifelong repercussions, and they're not always negative. Perhaps you know someone who grew, strengthened or awakened following a significant event that would've crushed most people. (I hope it was you.)

Our experiences have the power to create profound changes within us. One magnificent moment can change you for life, as often happens to new parents when their baby is born. Ironically, no experience rivals that kind of transformation quite like losing a loved one. Strangely enough, this book may never have been written if it wasn't for both the above events synchronising late last year.

It took one big life-changing and impactful experience to reignite my spirit enough to chase my dreams. After giving birth at 16 weeks, I learned that nothing tests your ability to sink or swim like the tidal waves of grief. We all love a comeback story because it proves that we can succeed despite life's most challenging circumstances. There truly is nothing life can throw at you that you cannot thrive in. Nowadays trauma to triumph and rags to riches stories aren't rare… They've become the norm!

*"Experience is a brutal teacher, but you learn.
My god, do you learn."*

- C.S. Lewis

Cycles and Experience

Like our cycles, experiences can be physical, mental or emotional, and they usually occur simultaneously. Although a cycle's 4mation always begins with an experience, it doesn't need to be direct or even your own. Some cycles formed because what happened to another person made you feel so strongly that you created beliefs and started acting on them. This can happen so fast that you don't even register it. Though it might sound odd, it occurs far more often than you'd think.

Let's say yesterday someone crawled through an open window and robbed a home in your neighbourhood. You are shocked by this story on the news and go to bed frightened and anxious. Alongside this emotional cycle, you're mentally spiralling with negative thoughts of how terrifying it would be and how you couldn't cope if this happened to you.

You start imagining a stranger breaking into your house to steal your belongings in the middle of the night while you're asleep. These inner cycles make you believe this will happen again, and soon. So now you keep your windows shut and doors locked, especially when you're home, so that no one can break in.

The 4mation of this cycle happened within a matter of minutes. You were collecting information during your **experience** of watching the news. You learned that robberies happen around you and it's

Element 3: Experiences

a risk to have open windows. This **knowledge** was powered by fear so it was **integrated** rapidly and the emotional cycle joined forces with a mental one. The belief was created that it'll happen again soon. You want to be sure it's not to you so keeping doors and windows locked was your **expression** of these cycles.

Expression is always related to physical actions. It can be something you say or do, but it could also be something you won't say or do instead (inaction). No matter what form it takes, it's simply the reflection of what you think and feel inside. It's important to note that not all cycles are fear-based, but a cycle's 4mation gets fast-tracked when you are fearful in an experience. This is because your survival mechanism focuses on emotion rather than logic and reason, which leads you to confuse possible with probable and spurs you into action.

You can repeat a physical cycle for years without ever connecting the original experience with your actions. We tend to mistake it as the problem, but mental and emotional cycles have more power over us than we give them credit for. They are ingrained in us far deeper than our physical cycles can ever be. Think about it. Your emotions and thoughts form first, are repeated the most and are the mysterious force behind everything you say and do, including the things you won't.

Physical cycles give the impression that they are more damaging as they are outer experiences, so we think that stopping them makes the problem go away. Almost all forms of our expression can be seen or heard, so we think that being in a toxic relationship or having money troubles is the issue. Sorry to tell you, but these are just the material manifestations of emotional and mental cycles. In other words, what you physically experience in life is the outer reflection of what's going on inside of you.

That's why soon after you leave that relationship or relieve that financial burden the issue miraculously reappears and you're facing a new toxic person and a different lot of expenses. When something keeps repeating in your life, you are seeing the *expression* of what lies at the core. Your mental and emotional cycles are where the *real* work must begin, or else the physical cycle will never stop!

This is why we fail fast when we suddenly try to stop online shopping, gambling, smoking or drinking. You're doomed if you make no effort to discover what's causing the problems you are sick and tired of experiencing. Only addressing the cycle that physically expresses your mental and emotional ones is like training for a marathon by simply preparing for the moment you cross the finish line. If your work doesn't even begin with a warm-up, what chance do you *really* have of ever completing the race?

You're not doing yourself any favours in the long run if you just target the symptom of a much deeper problem. Cold-turkey attempts to stop physical cycles are always short-lived because it's the hidden mental and emotional ones that must be broken for true success. So never forget that physical cycles are the *result* of an issue, not the actual cause of it.

You might believe things like insomnia, overeating, relationship issues and addictions are the problem, but they're just the symptoms. They point to the cycles underneath that are being expressed as the results you believe are your problems. The trick to breaking the physical part is to expose *them*. That's the most important step and (I'm not going to lie) the hardest one, but the good news is that gaining control over your physical cycles afterwards will be a piece of cake!

Element 3: Experiences

STUFF THAT SHOULD STICK

- Childhood and experiences form the super strand of your Web of Life.

- When you're going back into the past too often you're stuck in the rearview cycle, whereas the cycle of doom has you creating fear-based future scenarios that are unlikely to occur.

- Emotion dictates our perspective and our reaction - your awareness of this allows you greater control over how you view your experiences and how you feel about them.

- Judging others will always be inaccurate as you can only do so from the standpoint of your own web.

- Fear-based experiences enable the 4mation of negative cycles to be fast-tracked.

- An inside issue becomes visible outside of you with a cycle's expression, therefore they must be broken from the inside out and not the outside in!

CHAPTER 6

Element 4: Environment

This element has stronger repercussions on your health and well-being than all other elements combined. Your environment has the ability to influence every essential aspect of your life - it even has the power to modify your gene expression![1] From conception until your final breath, this element is the most fundamental factor in determining a wide-range of vital outcomes for you, including your very survival. This is one of many reasons why it is said that we are all products of our environment.[2]

It's where we take our cues from, which guides how we (and our genes) behave. So it shouldn't come as a shock, but your environment is where you were introduced to cycles and where many of yours were inflicted on you.

The Foundation Strand

Your first experiences of life started with this fundamental element and its counterpart, relationships. These two are the foundation strand of your Web of Life. Though your web began to be woven before you were conceived, you started weaving it yourself during the prenatal period. Your mother's womb was the only physical environment you knew before you were born, and that's also the place that your first relationship began to develop.

The bond between you and your mother was so deeply intense that you actually felt her stress and moods. This means you were first introduced to cycles by sharing your mother's emotional ones with her. Her emotional state and connection to you throughout pregnancy was the predominant energy you experienced in your first home and in your first relationship. Talk about foundations!

Element 4: Environment

These two elements also share a special connection because they are the foundation for each other's existence. Think about this for a second. Your environments provide opportunities for your relationships to form. You had to go to school to make those friends as a child, right? Ever refer to someone as a work friend?

We stick these two elements together to identify the people in our lives. We even name the place before the person so others know exactly where we met. The bond would never have existed without it! You see, everything in our lives happens alongside a relationship and all experiences occur within an environment. Technically a relationship is an environment in and of itself. It's no wonder that young children view the world as an environment of relationships.[3]

Human Habitats

How can I possibly define such a broad and all-encompassing element in your Web of Life? I wouldn't know how to, so I'll leave it to one of the greats!

> *"The environment is everything that isn't me."*
>
> *- Albert Einstein*

The field of psychology agrees, considering the environment to be any outside forces that you're influenced by.[4] You see, an inflicted cycle is an outside force, and you know that negative cycles wreak havoc on your life. So it was your environments and the people in them that determined which cycles you were introduced to as you grew up.

Perhaps you're familiar with the cycles of blame, criticism, codependence or competition. At the time you're so affected by them that you create cycles to cope, while spending the rest of your life trying to avoid making the inflicted ones your own. But when an environmental cycle is all you've ever known, repeating it yourself happens quite naturally. This is good news if your surroundings were positive, supportive and nurturing, but who on Earth only ever experienced nothing but good places and people?

We pick up many cycles from our environments. This began as kids in the place we called home. Having a secure and safe environment where we're around emotionally available adults is crucial, though we had no choice in what or who we got.

Hopefully home was your refuge but maybe it was more like a warzone you wanted to flee from like a refugee. Those who had bad experiences at home may still be struggling to break the cycles they created to survive. Growing up in a happy home doesn't mean you don't have negative cycles in this element, it just means the bug wasn't caught in that particular environment.

Environmental Cycles

The predominant environmental cycles we get stuck in revolve around how we react to our surroundings and the experiences we have within them. They tend to function in some way and on some level for all of us. The most popular two are like fireworks; just when you think they're finished, the next one is about to pop off. These cycles just start going off at specific stages in life too, and identifying the bug (core experience) that started it can be tricky. You may not notice when you're stuck in either of these cycles, but those closest to you will see it clear as day.

Element 4: Environment

The cycle of change might sound positive and uplifting, but it has the opposite effect on your life. It's based on happiness but always keeps it at a distance, so you are forever on the chase. I was in a relationship with someone stuck in this cycle. He had this belief that he'd be happy once he reached a higher status or level in our relationship. He was never content and kept expecting the next stage or step forward in life to bring him happiness.

There were massive fireworks going off yearly like it was New Year's Eve and still, it made no difference. It was never enough. It didn't matter how his life progressed or how much things changed, he didn't appreciate what he had or where he was. He just wanted more. This had a negative impact on his sense of self-worth and ultimately, our relationship.

I noticed it was first expressed when he said, "I'll be happy when we live together". Then it was, "I'll be happy when we have our own place. I'll be happy when we're engaged… When we get married". It wasn't until he said "I'll be happy when we have children" that finally I realised this cycle was without end.

Whenever he'd get the change he wanted there was no satisfaction, just the desire for the next thing. Yet he would still think the next thing would bring him happiness. Me? I was always happy with each new experience of our lives and in our relationship… especially when we got divorced!

> *"Happiness is determined more by one's state of mind than by external events."*
>
> *- Dalai Lama, The Art of Happiness*

Have you ever thought that you'd be happy once things have changed? When your environment changes or your relationships with the people in it change? Maybe when you change jobs, move to a better area, buy a new car, get a bigger house or go on a holiday. The cycle of change manifests in different ways, but is usually based on material possessions or specific accomplishments.

The keyword is 'when' and the key phrase is 'I'll be happy'. In between the two lay your desires, which is basically just more of what you already have. More money, more security, more space, more stuff, more stability or more status. When success in any endeavour is your measure of happiness, you're playing with fire. Letting external circumstances decide your internal state leaves you wide open for third degree burns.

The trap of this cycle is the belief that you can't be happy *until* things change, which causes two unavoidable side effects. You confuse what you want with what you need and then once you get what you want the next thing you "need" magically appears. You will always be chasing happiness thinking it'll come after the next set of fireworks. Meanwhile, the smoke is still settling from the last one, yet you don't feel any different.

Unlike the one that keeps you pushing for change, the cycle of stagnation is the total opposite. You resist change altogether and prefer (or demand) that everything stay the same. After all, life is just easier that way.

This cycle keeps you permanently in your comfort zone as you're usually too anxious to leave it. No reason is good enough to even try. Just thinking about something (or someone) being different than you're used to makes you anxious.

Element 4: Environment

People stuck in this cycle can't cope with change very well, especially when it's big, happens fast or there are multiple things changing at once. If you're given the opportunity to say no to something new, you will. You will still say no when you don't have a say or a choice in the matter. You will even fight against changes that have nothing to do with you.

The cycle of stagnation is in full swing not just when you prefer to play it safe, but when you *have* to keep doing what you know and what works easily for you. The idea of adapting or adjusting makes you uncomfortable and unhappy. Routine is likely to be your middle name and the saying 'creature of habit' fits you to a tee!

Stagnation is a fear-based cycle that makes you afraid of the unknown, so you never change it up. This cycle limits your potential for growth and stifles your self-development. You struggle to challenge yourself with unfamiliar things and refuse anything outside of what is considered 'normal' for you. This goes for accepting other people's choices too.

Though these fireworks are more obvious in older people, there are many ways in which this cycle manifests in everyday life for all of us. Yes, you too. Maybe you stay in a job where you are unhappy and undervalued but think, better the devil you know. Who's to say I will be happier at a new one anyway?

Perhaps you're in a long-term relationship that has run its course, but you feel uncertain you can find someone else. So you stay put because being alone isn't even an option. Now that I've showed you some subtle ways this cycle is expressed, reflect on how you may be perpetuating this cycle in your life.

Toxic Environments

I'm sure you know what a toxic environment is, but have you personally experienced one? Was it at home? At school? At work? In a relationship? Unhealthy environments invade both your inner and outer worlds, so what you experienced was mirrored inside of you. What you saw, heard and felt would immediately shift your mood.

It's akin to living in a natural disaster zone, except these harsh living conditions can only be caused by other human beings. The impacts on you are just as rapid and extreme as the worst events on Earth, and they can be just as deadly. Sadly, some people prefer to take their own life rather than continue to subject themselves to the torment.

A toxic environment is like living in a tornado, it's a whirlwind of emotional devastation and mental destruction. Meanwhile you're in constant anticipation of the inevitable volcanic eruptions that vary in proportion. You're also fearful of the magnitude of the next earthquake because you're still being hit by the tsunami from the last one. Those waves of hurt, dread and defeat are relentless.

Just thinking about what's to come will send aftershocks through your entire body. If it sounds difficult and dangerous to escape a toxic environment, that's because it is! Though some people are stuck in a vicious cycle where they go from one to another, it actually requires a cycle of its own to function.

Violence is one of the most common, and unfortunately this one can also be generational. You may have personally experienced this cycle, or you know someone who has. It is a trauma endured by many people around the world. Just in Australia, 2.5 million adults have declared they experienced physical abuse during their childhood.[5] When I met Anastasia I discovered why this environmental cycle is repeated so easily by the next generation.

Anastasia was raised in a household with domestic and family violence. It was never talked about or shared with others, so each family member was left to their own devices to cope. This meant that as a child she learned to function within the dysfunction. So she got comfortable with the chaos and violence was normalised in family life. The infliction of this cycle was enough for her to allow it to continue into her intimate relationships as an adult.

Although she hated this part of her childhood and resented her mother for staying, she could never bring herself to leave violent men. She believed violence was a normal part of conflict in relationships so she was quick to accept it. In fact, she had almost come to expect it.

Once this cycle began with a new partner, those that she'd created to cope in her childhood just naturally took over. The main one was the cycle of appearances. As the violence was kept a family secret, her instinct was to hide the truth and pretend her relationship was happy and healthy.

But to enable the cycle of violence to continue in her relationship other cycles had to revolve too. In Anastasia's case, her partner pushed the cycle of unworthiness to resurface. Though she'd started to break it a year earlier, her partner was able to reverse her hard work rather quickly. With a conscious effort perhaps she could've stopped this old cycle from going full circle again, but it's extremely difficult to override when someone else is forcing its repetition.

Like many stuck in this cycle she wanted to stay in the relationship. She just wanted the violence to stop. The problem is that apologies and promises will always be made, whereas the changes that are needed won't. Detangling their web shows you how they became the person they are and why they do what they do. Although it doesn't justify their behaviour, understanding their cycles will give you the greatest chance to support them in breaking them. That is, if they want to.

Now it's important to say this directly and emphatically - you *cannot* break a cycle for another person! It takes courage, dedication, vulnerability and true strength. At best you can be their sidekick, but only if they're willing and committed to being their own superhero.

Power Plays

Though you are significantly influenced by your environment, it doesn't hold all of the power. Think about how a 2-year-old's temper tantrum impacts the space they occupy and anyone within a 20-metre radius! Yes, at will and with intention, you can directly influence your environment. This means you have the power to make changes when it no longer serves you.

You see, the beauty of Einstein's definition is that it reminds us of our innate power over our surroundings. You are the greatest force for change in your life and you have the potential to make anything happen. As for everything that isn't you? Well, if you have loving intentions and practice gratitude regardless of your external environment, measurable improvements will occur inside your mind and body. So always remember that your outer world doesn't hold a candle to the power of your inner one.

Element 4: Environment

STUFF THAT SHOULD STICK

- Environment and relationships form the foundation strand of your Web of Life.

- The cycles of change and stagnation are polar opposites, yet we can be simultaneously stuck in both at the same time about different things (or people) in our lives.

- Toxic environments are cyclical in nature but can be a cycle in and of itself, with some people bouncing from one to another.

- You cannot break another person's cycle or make them do it if they're not ready to put in the work to understand the hows and whys of their own behaviour.

CHAPTER 7

Element 5: Childhood

Have you ever wished you could be a kid again?

The imprint childhood leaves on you is deep and everlasting. The memories are prominent and the programming is potent. As it is your beginning it is the most formative time of your life, moulding the very core of you. No other life-stage is as critical to your growth and development, which is one of many reasons why this element is fundamental to us all.

Making Sense of the Self

Your childhood is where the groundwork was laid for your self-confidence, self-esteem and self beliefs. However you weren't the one setting the tone for the future you. That happened behind the scenes with those in your social sphere. You actually began to develop your self-knowledge through your exposure to the comments and criticisms of others. How you were spoken to and about as a child started to shape your self-perception, which is why you may still find remnants of this in your self-talk as an adult.

How often do you repeat something negative about yourself that came from someone else? Maybe it's just in your head or you say it aloud. Regardless, those expressions are the result of a self-sphere cycle from your childhood. Probably the first one you ever created.

The 4mation of the mental and emotional parts occurred when you experienced someone you knew saying negative things about you. This was usually based on comments about your abilities or perceived lack thereof, name-calling, labels or criticisms. Often it was parental figures, siblings, relatives, friends or teachers whose words left a lifelong mark, but the social sphere includes coaches, pastors and more.

Element 5: Childhood

You were just a child gaining knowledge about yourself and the world when you were told some very specific information. Although it was circumstantial at best, it was presented to you as factual. So as a kid not knowing any better, you integrated it into your developing self-concept, which kickstarted the inner cycles.

Regardless of whether you heard it once or a thousand times, those childhood voices echoed in your mind for so long that the words became a self-belief. Then, just like Tim back in Chapter 3, those inner cycles will push their way out of you. No matter what form it took, the first time it was expressed the 4mation of this childhood cycle was complete. How long it continued and how strong it became afterwards, however, was totally up to you

The words from one experience as a child with someone you had a relationship with was enough to inform your beliefs for a lifetime. The power of the three anchor elements is truly undeniable when you reflect on this cycle. The fact that most of us still repeat it shows that our strongest ones began as children, which explains why they're so hard to break. However experience has taught me that the ways we express childhood cycles get far more self-destructive than just repeating negative phrases from our past.

Family Matters

When I was young, all 20 relatives on my mother's side of the family would pile into my grandmother's three-bedroom beach house for holidays. Mattresses replaced the living room floor and a tent was pitched in the backyard for the overflow. Come dinnertime, Nonna made enough gnocchi to feed an army, so we'd overeat, drink and laugh around tables across two rooms.

In memory of Nonno, we'd mix wine with lemonade to recreate his famous "strawberry" drink. Once our bellies were bloated and the burping began, so did the real fun! My cousins and I would leap from couch to couch, trying to escape being eaten by the shark lurking in the mattress ocean.

I rarely think of times like these. Occasionally when similar stories are shared by others they might gently reemerge. Yet rather than reminisce, I'll tell them my story to connect with theirs. The memories I'd rather forget, on the other hand, are forever burned into my brain. No matter how much I've tried to forgive or forget, share or suppress, heal or help it, they've always haunted me.

Particularly these ones.

My parents were playing in the pool with their friends when my 2-year-old brother fell in. I tried desperately to get their attention and help, but my panicked screams were drowned out for so long he lost consciousness.

My splash caught everyone's attention. But I'd dragged his lifeless body up the stairs and out of the pool by the time they reached us. Through their legs I watched as he was given chest compressions, and had lost all hope when he finally coughed up water and opened his eyes.

The next afternoon my mother told me I did a very brave thing. As she hyped up a reward that could buy me anything I wanted my mind trailed off, thinking about my coming million. I was puzzled by the price paid for saving his life. I knew his funeral would have cost more than a dollar, as would my parent's grief. I guess she must've just assumed I was too young to have any idea about the value, of money or of life. The only thing I was clueless about was what all of this was going to cost me.

I started to find out a few days later when I told my cousins. With shock and excitement they rushed outside to where our mothers were talking and shared the news. I followed with a proud smile that disappeared with the look my mother shot me. I stood in disbelief as she denied it and told them I was a liar before casually continuing her conversation with her sister.

This was my introduction to the cycle of appearances. At 4 years old I learned there was no limit to the sacrifices people are willing make to protect their image. Then over the next 30 years I discovered the extraordinary lengths people go to to hide the truth and maintain it. My mother also let me down again later that year, except those screams being ignored resulted in me becoming sexually active. I was in kindergarten.

> *"Children don't get traumatised because they are hurt. They get traumatised because they're alone with the hurt."*
>
> *- Gabor Maté*

The ways I have buried these painful memories aren't half as bad as what I did *with* them. Or rather, what they did with me. I didn't realise I was giving them any kind of power when I defined myself by them, but it's an easy trap to fall into. Little did I know this would also start the worst cycle I would ever come to know. And the hardest ever broken.

The Cycle of Victimhood

Having faced those situations alone was more than enough evidence to really get this cycle rolling. The mental and emotional parts pegged me as the victim, proven by what I'd gone through and my mother's actions (and lack thereof). So as a child the knowledge I integrated from those experiences was:

1. The world was against me

2. I'll always be on my own

3. I am powerless to change 1 and 2

These 'facts' led me to believe that not only was I the victim, but that suffering was inescapable. It took near total self-destruction to realise that this colossal mistake enabled this cycle to take over my entire life.

The worst part is that it took next to nothing for me to repeat it. I'd spiral internally in a matter of seconds whenever I faced anything even remotely challenging. As soon as an experience brought on the *here we go again* feeling I would think *this always happens to me*. Any kind of expression in physical form would then complete the cycle and further solidify it in my web.

At first it was saying 'story of my life' out loud in the face of opposition and obstacles, or when the feeling of defeat was too overwhelming I would just avoid them altogether. But as the cycle strengthened inside of me over time, so did the ways it came out.

When your world view is narrowed to see only victims and villains, your mind becomes adept at detecting them. When I learned about historical atrocities in school it quickly established this as a global problem. Victims were everywhere; Aboriginal people, the planet, the foster kid in my class. The lens of suffering through which I saw life was also reflected in the way I retold stories, particularly my own. But by high school this cycle had control of far more than just my perspective.

Element 5: Childhood

Though it might sound strange, the main form of expression came through my posture. I didn't do it consciously, as is often the case with the physical part of the trifecta. It was as if I tried to protect myself from being hurt again, slouched over with my head down and rounded shoulders. There were other subtle expressions similar to this too, like being less feminine and more masculine.

Keep in mind that many physical expressions are tied to the inner parts of a cycle, but it rarely ever begins with big or obvious behaviours. In fact, sometimes a cycle will never manifest into any major physical actions whatsoever, and there will always be those created in fear that only result in forms of inaction like avoidance. In saying this, don't underestimate the power of subtle expressions or idleness to cause you long-term damage. I'm still trying to correct my posture in my mid-thirties.

This cycle wasn't just expressed in what I did, but also precisely what I wouldn't. Like wear tight-fitting and revealing clothes. Or trust anyone. Never being vulnerable was my shield and unyielding strength was my sword. It was me against the world. I would say and do hurtful things, thinking not to appear weak was self-preservation. It wasn't. It was self-sabotage. My tough exterior may have masked my pain and fear, but it cost me friendships, peace and the best parts of my personality. I hated the person I had become.

So the time was ripe for my escapism and self-loathing streak to meet substances. Cue an introduction to cigarettes and boom - the relationship took off like a rocket! Alcohol made some guest appearances at social events, not that smoking really needed a supporting act. The blackouts were welcomed but I got over it soon after I met Mary Jane.

If marijuana was my gateway, then trauma walked me directly to it. I experimented with other things too, but smoking weed would suppress the inner cycles so I could sleep. It worked like a charm until everything started to surface in my early twenties, screaming to come out. Suddenly my pain could no longer be numbed and I could no longer contain it. Eventually I stopped sleeping altogether and my addiction went way past the point where most people go to rehab. But still, I kept going.

I ended up institutionalised a few times in a system some people can never be free of. Encouraged by my mother telling nurses my emotions fluctuate and I hallucinate childhood traumas, labels like psychotic and bipolar were tossed around. I fought like hell against medications that would've rendered me docile everyday and infertile for life.

I had a choice - continue destroying myself with recreational drugs, or the next hospitalisation would force it with pharmaceutical ones. This decision gave me the clarity to see that the cycle of victimhood required fuel in order to repeat. But there was no way that substances could've been that power supply because I hadn't used them my whole life. The only source that could be relied upon to feed energy to a negative cycle was another one!

This sudden awareness brought about a life-altering realisation - that victimhood *needs* validation. But the problem with this cycle is that no one can avoid its infliction because it's embedded into childhood.

Even if yours was perfect.

The Cycle of Validation

All we really want in life is for people to affirm our truths, accept our emotions and recognise the worthiness of our opinions. This is why telling your story as an adult is the predominant form of expression for childhood cycles. We desire to be heard, felt, understood and connected with, so we share what we have gone through in an effort to seek validation for our pain and suffering.

As children, the majority of us weren't able to be open and freely share our deepest struggles. We were hardly free to openly express our emotions as we weren't able to be properly supported through them. So as we progressed from childhood into adolescence, we'd learned to bury far more than we showed. Without a voice for our pain or an outlet for its impacts, all the suppressed secrets and emotions of the past start to rise up.

Rather than keep pushing them down and pretending you're ok, it's easier to rely on things outside of you to change how you feel inside altogether. Teenagers don't have to reach very far for substances, so for me using them was a no-brainer. The problem was that two addictions formed though I was only aware of one. Everything changed once I realised that my substance addiction was also an addiction to validating my victimhood.

The victimhood cycle was mostly expressed through trauma responses, such as mistrust and sleep disturbances. But each time that cycle became physical it simultaneously kickstarted the cycle of validation. So the urge I'd get to *do something* to take the edge off my edginess was the end of one cycle and the start of another. Victimhood was the front wheels and validation was the back, revolving together and driving me, the vehicle, straight off a cliff.

These two can be entangled quite easily because we all grow up with the cycle of validation. It's such a normal part of daily life for a child that we never even notice it exists. The fact that it's present in every environment not only allows it to function under the radar, but ensures that we perpetuate it in our own lives unaware of what we're actually doing.

Do you realise how many essential aspects of your childhood had to be validated by an adult? Any outburst had an adult deciding if there was an issue and whether it was worthy of your emotional response. Disagreements were cross-checked to determine if your argument had any merit and choose the outcome. Your presentation, expression, attitude, effort, ideas and communication were constantly scrutinised by the adults around you. Everything you felt, thought, said and did required acceptance and approval. At home it was a parent. At school it was a teacher. On the field it was a coach.

Now don't get me wrong, I'm not saying adults shouldn't oversee things for children. But the problem is too often the validity of a child's thoughts and emotions are shut down by adults unwilling to deal with them - mostly because they don't know how to. As this cycle is inflicted on each generation by the last, parental unavailability and incapacity becomes inherently expected; which is exactly why we must break this generational cycle.

As Dr. Bruce Lipton explains, our experiences between gestation and six years of age create the most powerful programs in our subconscious minds.[6] This influence is often described as conditioning. So how would the cycle of validation repeating across all your environments impact you? It would program your subconscious mind to value the approval of others higher than your own, and condition you to go against your intuition and instincts.

Element 5: Childhood

How any of us can develop a strong sense of self afterwards is a miracle! How could we learn self-approval when we were always told if we were right or wrong, good or bad, telling the truth or lies by someone else?

Rather than be free to discover your authentic self this cycle pressured you to meet the expectations of others. You had to oblige to keep yourself liked and validated, though it's possible you *had* to keep those around you happy for your own safety and protection. As it was inflicted everywhere you went this cycle frequently invalidated your true nature and set the stage for you to keep transforming into who everyone else wanted you to be.

Clearly this cycle created issues for the *real* you because being accepted as someone you're not forces you to disconnect from yourself. So you had to suppress the part of you that was seen as unacceptable, which enabled people pleasing to become your normal way of life. What could've possibly been more limiting (or damaging) to your self-expression as a child?

Though it was first inflicted upon you, eventually you started self-inflicting this cycle. Yet, like people pleasing, you probably didn't know you were doing it! The biggest red flag is seeking validation from others about what you think, feel, say and do. Do you ever ask people if your opinion of a person is accurate? How about questioning whether or not your actions in a situation are justified? Do you check if you're right to feel the way you do, about an issue or a person? How often do you ask others if you look ok? We do this sort of thing *all* the time, and this potent cycle is why!

It seems totally innocent, but asking for validation indicates that the mental and emotional parts of this cycle have spun out of control. What's going on inside you begs to be expressed and asking for support is the dead giveaway that it has been! Now asking for advice is one thing... but *approval* is another. Being conditioned by this cycle since childhood really makes me wonder if we are even capable of distinguishing between the two.

You see, the mental cycle is needing to know what others think and feel. The emotional cycle is ever-present uncertainty about your own thoughts, feelings and actions. Then the physical cycle keeps you actively seeking out validation from others. This is why people thrive off likes and comments on social media nowadays.

Though this cycle can reach beyond the social sphere and into the world sphere thanks to the internet, it's actually more dangerous to keep it in the self sphere. As the methods of self-infliction available to you only increase as you get older, this means the risks are heightened. Usually this remains unnoticed until it's too late and you've completely lost control, which allows the cycle to take over your life. That certainly was the case for me and you may not have noticed it before, but it might also be the case for you too.

You may be perpetuating the cycle of validation without realising as it tends to operate without your conscious awareness. Say you had a tough week so you stop off to get some wine on the way home from work. Why not? You deserve it, right? Maybe you go to the pub for Friday night drinks with some work mates instead and while you're there you gamble a bit. You earned it, didn't you? So what's the harm in blowing off some steam... and a couple hundred bucks!

Perhaps your style is to buy junk food, get take-away for dinner, binge a brain-numbing series, shop online or get laid. Your expression of this cycle may look different, but it doesn't matter what you physically do because mentally and emotionally we are all spiralling around the same thing. The truth is there *is* no difference whether you are buying stuff, consuming crap or injecting methamphetamines. The fact remains that you are doing *something* to validate a negative experience, and feeding energy to this cycle only strengths it! So every time you feel that urge and satisfy it, you complete the cycle and propel it back into motion!

This cycle operates so secretly inside you that by the time you spring into action you are totally misguided about the problem. It's not your day, your life, your relationship, your work or stress that made you do it. It's the mental and emotional cycles of validation fuelling your need to express them.

That's why you feel like you have to physically *do something*. Tell someone, have a drink, a smoke, gamble, buy something. It comes out in all kinds of addictive behaviours that get out of hand. It might even be a form of physical expression you don't think is connected, such as aggression or anxiety. So unbeknownst to you, every time you complete the cycle you are not only validating your negative experience, but your victimhood as well.

Big Ts and Little Ts

Given the opportunity, almost everyone will reveal something significant from their childhood that's had a devastating and lifelong impact on them. This is the time that shapes us all the most and presents us with many of the experiences that we spiral around for the rest of our lives. So to completely understand yourself (or anyone else for that matter), it's clear you must detangle the bugs in your Web of Life starting from this powerful period.

It's undeniable that these wounds take the longest to heal and their scars will always remain. Whether it was a big trauma or a bunch of little ones, having our pain validated by others makes up for the invalidation we received as children and helps us along our path to healing. Though the impacts of trauma vary over time and from person to person, one thing is certain; it creates a series of cycles that, if left unchecked, will continue for the rest of your life.

Element 5: Childhood

STUFF THAT SHOULD STICK

- The YOU self that you *think* you are now was created in your mind from a young age, built upon other people's opinions and comments about you.

- This forms the basis of your self-beliefs and perception about *who you are;* which spawns your first ever self-sphere belief cycles and the hardcore ones that likely still linger, despite years of opposition and extensive evidence, mind you!

- The cycle of validation is a generational one that operates in every childhood environment. It programs you to seek other's approval and applies the pressure to conform to outside expectations (especially those of authority figures like parents, but also includes social expectations).

- The cycle of victimhood and the cycle of validation are ALWAYS connected - validation without victimhood doesn't mean you're free and clear of victimhood as your desire for acceptance makes you victim to comments, opinions, critique, feedback and criticisms of others.

- The cycle of validation is repeatedly revolving for the majority of us and we constantly continue to perpetuate it. The catch is that it's hard to recognise how often you're perpetuating it, even when you know it exists as a cycle in your web.

CHAPTER 8

Element 6: History

History is everywhere. It's in the stories of First Nations peoples and religions of the world. In the teachings of the mystics and the sages. In our art and performances on stages and screens.

It's in the plaques and statues on the streets and in parks. In the architecture of landmarks, bridges and buildings. In the special celebrations and commemorative holidays in the calendar each year.

It's also preserved in nature throughout our beautiful planet. We see it in ancient tree rings and sea floor sediments. In the Earth's core and the layers of ice sheets. Whether you are stargazing or looking out across a mountain range, history is encoded in everything.

It's in your genes and cells, which is why you resemble a family member and how your ancestry can be traced back to its original location. Your personal history is actually much larger than the story of your life and, as you will soon discover, it also expands further than the life stories of all family members, even going back several generations.

The Time Strand

In the first chapter you learned that beliefs and history share a fundamental connection. As these two elements endure through the ages they form the time strand of your Web of Life. The collective histories and beliefs of your ancestors are contained here, as are the residues of their traumas as they too have the power to transcend time.

If your past continues to affect your life, then you can appreciate that this would also have been the case for your parents and their parents alike. But when do these affects disappear? Do they leave without a trace at some point in time or are they imprinted in some way upon the next generation?

Remnants of the past will always live on and in some ways they must. Without this generational exchange culture and tradition would not survive, although some of the beliefs passed down in the process cause more harm than good. After all, it is the time strand that's responsible for the prevalence of discrimination, prejudice, violence and oppression. Therefore to best explore this element and its implications we must first zoom out and look inwards at your web from the furthest vantage point.

The World Sphere

History played the most vital role in shaping the lives of those that came before you. Global events including war, genocide and colonisation drastically impacted previous generations and determined many important outcomes for their lives. Those experiences were clearly woven into the webs of your ancestors, however some of them were also entangled within your own.

For example, my parents would never have been in the same country to meet if it wasn't for events on the other side of the world. War and poverty drove my mother's parents out of Italy as teenagers seeking more opportunity, meanwhile a coup in Egypt forced my father and his parents out of the country as they were Greek. Circumstances elsewhere in the world may have resulted in similar outcomes for your ancestors, so those experiences are woven into this element of your web.

As history changed the course of many lives it's necessary to reflect on how it impacted your family lineage. You'd be surprised how much of the past has direct implications for your Web of Life. If your ancestors were prevented from migration or travel, this restricted marriages to families in the same village, tribe or province. Like me, without the occurrence of certain events, maybe you would never have been born, or perhaps you would've been raised in another country and be speaking a different language now.

History also significantly influenced culture and tradition, so it's important to consider how this affected the life choices and opportunities of your ascendants. Many relationships were forbidden due to conflicting values such as class, religion, race, ethnicity and social status. Being that marriage was determined by these factors historically, couples who defied the social and cultural expectations of the time were forced to leave and start a new life. So you might be related to some of the world's first generational cycle breakers or you might be alive right now specifically because your relatives continued that cycle.

Our family lineage is integral to our history and our ancestors actually lived through the major world events that are taught in school. These events have left us with a legacy of problematic cycles, many of which we are still trying to overcome. Therefore to grasp an understanding of what is woven into the history element of your Web of Life it's crucial to consider the cascading impacts of your ancestor's life experiences.

> *"Who has fully realised that history is not contained in thick books but lives in our very own blood?"*
>
> *- Carl Jung*

The Social Sphere

A tsunami builds over time as it travels across water, but the epicentre is far from where the wave hits the shore. The same is true for generational cycles. They started long ago in a distant place and have gained power and momentum from multiple generations repeating them. So you must always consider the possibility that a cycle was passed down for a century or more before it was inflicted upon you.

Therefore there's a chance that the cycles you experienced at home as a child didn't start with your parents. We don't tend to think further than them as the source, but the point of origin could just as easily have been with our grandparents. A cycle may have even began in a different (probably more harsh) variation, generations before them.

You can appreciate that the cycles of your grandparents were introduced to them by their own parents, and so on and so fourth. This is how generational cycles come into being. They start at home during childhood and are normalised with repetition. Depending upon the time in history your family members grew up, cycles might have also been perpetuated in other social environments too.

For example, physical punishment and violence was as much a part of education as it was the home life for many of our oldest relatives. From this perspective you can understand how history has created many of the cycles that some countries, communities, cultures and families are still trying to break. This is the legacy of history and explains why it repeats itself - it revolves in cycles!

To help you uncover the origins of generational cycles in your web you need to know about your ancestors' environments and their experiences within them. The details of their lives may not be known about or openly shared in your family, but their histories shaped your environments. Think about this. The home you grew up in was influenced by the experiences both your parents had in their own homes as children, which was a byproduct of history at that time. The same is true for each of your grandparents' childhood homes.

But as major historical events like war significantly impacted your grandparents' or great grandparents' lives, those affects would've been reflected in their home environments and in the experiences their children had. So just as belief cycles are repeated over time, environmental cycles can be repeated in families.

Yet it goes far deeper than this. The truth is that the painful experiences of family members can actually create their own historical cycles. The effects of trauma being passed down generations is known as inherited family trauma and Mark Wolynn shares the latest groundbreaking research on this phenomenon in his book *It didn't start with you: How inherited family trauma shapes who we are and how to end the cycle*.

We hear regularly that time heals all wounds and assume it refers to one lifetime, but it turns out there is compelling evidence to the contrary. Pain caused by trauma can remain alive when the original sufferer has passed on or when their story has been buried for years. Throughout his 25 years of experience working with patients suffering from conditions ranging from depression, chronic pain and PTSD to phobias and obsessive thoughts, Wolynn observed a deep connection between trauma and language.[7]

He found that what lay at the core of these conditions would surface in everyday language, so he examined the thoughts and emotions behind the words of his patients. Many of their issues were rooted in early childhood trauma or, more interestingly, trauma in the family history. Memories, sensations and fragmented experiences of past traumas would appear in other family members, sometimes two or three generations later.

Believing that these mental, emotional or physical experiences were surfacing in order to finally be healed, Wolynn formulated the Core Language Approach®, an innovative method to help people overcome anxiety and fear.[8] One of his clients was a 39-year-old woman named Gretchen who'd had strong suicidal urges since she was a teenager. When she explained her plan to kill herself he was alarmed by the terms she used to describe it.

The words *vaporise* and *incinerate* reminded him of his work with families affected by the Holocaust, so he asked if she had any Jewish ancestors. It turned out that her grandmother had lost her entire family in Auschwitz. They were gassed with poisonous vapours before they were incinerated in the oven.[9] Gretchen's suicidal ideations were clearly rooted in a family cycle of trauma inherited from her grandmother.

Now you are probably wondering if this is really possible. Let me assure you, not only is it possible, but scientists can actually prove trauma has been passed down and explain how it happens! But we'll explore the emerging research behind this alluring topic in the science element.

The Self Sphere

Your personal history has made you who you are so it was likely the first thing to come to mind when it came to this chapter. It's your Web of Life after all. History is a comprehensive record of the past, so there is no denying that yours is crucial to understanding yourself. However this element concerns the underlying connection between your ancestors' experiences and your own, so we must consider the self sphere quite differently here. This is necessary because, as you will now discover, your existence greatly predates your conception.

Embryology can trace your earliest biological form back to when your grandmother was five months pregnant with your mother. At this time the egg that you developed from was a precursor cell in your mother's ovaries. So as you shared the same environment, technically three generations existed within the one body.[10] This has some profound implications that we will cover when we explore the science element.

This ancestral connection is practically mirrored in your paternal lineage too. When your father was a fetus in his mother's womb, the precursor cells you developed from were already present in him. Now science tells us that events can imprint both precursor sperm and egg cells, which means the traumas your parents experienced had the potential to impact you before you were even conceived.

According to the latest advancements in neuroscience, cellular biology and epigenetics among other fields, to grasp an understanding of these recurring cycles it's crucial to investigate a minimum of three generations of family history.[11] So I implore you to do the same level of inquiry for this element in your Web of Life. Evidently traumas can create historical cycles that are woven into the webs of future generations.

You can start by exploring your parents' history and try weaving their webs as you might find that you can gain clarity on some of your own experiences. It certainly helped me make sense of a particularly painful part of my childhood. Despite our troubled relationship it always hurt whenever my mother called me a selfish and ungrateful bitch. As it happened often I'd forever be questioning what I did wrong, but this knowledge was quickly integrated into my self beliefs.

Whilst exploring her relationship history with my grandmother I learned the origin of these words. They were screamed at her father during an emotionally disturbing experience in her own childhood (albeit bitch was replaced with bastard). The story behind it alerted me to a powerful truth that could finally put me on the path to forgiveness; it was the infliction of a historical cycle. And it turns out they're actually quite common.

I've been told countless stories of parents hurling insults at their children. The spectrum is incredibly vast, from name-calling, labelling and comparing one child to another to blaming them for ruining their lives or marriages. But regardless of the content in the insult, those experiences gave them information that was integrated into their developing self-knowledge. However as Wolynn explains, the core language points to past traumas that are seeking to be resolved.[12]

You see, it comes out as an infliction but parental insults are the physical expression of a cycle that began long ago. Perhaps they were repeating phrases that were said to them as children or saying what they had always wanted to but never could. Maybe, as was the case for my mother, it's an entrenched belief that was only able to be shared once. However, as we now know, it's also possible that they were the residue of traumas experienced by another generation altogether.

This is why it's important to explore the relationship histories in your family. Parent to parent, each parent to each child, each sibling to the other, family to family and so on and so forth. This exercise is particularly helpful if, like me, you had a complicated relationship with a parent, sibling or extended relative. Finding connections (or cycles) between past and present relationships can provide insight into your own experiences and pave your way to forgiveness as it did for me.

Wolynn also discovered that different degrees of tragedy can send shockwaves down family lines. This includes war, suicide, abandonment and the untimely death of children, siblings or parents.[13] When I detangled my grandparents' webs I was surprised to find two historical cycles. Going back three generations on one side of my family the first child was always conceived outside of wedlock. Granted it didn't bring any shame, social stigma or disadvantage to the child born in the current generation, but it certainly had ramifications for previous ones.

However on the other side of my family is a much more devastating cycle that also relates to children but, ironically, sits on the opposite end of the spectrum. The first child of five women over three generations was lost due to medical misfortune. No matter the method the result was the same; grief. Stillborn, illness, miscarriage and termination have pervaded my family. In my grandmother's case, it was the death of four children in every way but the last. It turned out to be me who would experience the latter at the end of 2021.

No one aims to recreate their negative experiences for others and the same is true for generational cycles. In fact, I've never met a living soul who intended to pass them on. Parents want their children to have better lives than they did, and believe they will so long as they don't repeat their parents' mistakes. But it's much easier said than done.

Element 6: History

Breaking a generational cycle requires one to take steps they were never shown and walk paths never before seen. Given these circumstances most of us would fall short, which is why parents usually end up distilling generational cycles into unique, more subdued versions with their children. The idea that parents did the best they could do signifies the harsh reality - that historical cycles simply got the better of them.

It's not their fault, though. They have to contend with biological imprints of the past and the effects of their own life experiences starting from childhood. In addition, there has never been a complete guide for parents to understand themselves and their cycles, let alone a book to explain how they're broken. That is, until now.

The Mechanics Behind Your Foundation

As you are aware your Web of Life began with three fundamental elements. Beliefs, relationships and experiences are the anchor points that formed its basic structure. However there are three other elements that are responsible for creating these foundations. To understand what I mean, imagine the creation of your web like the construction of an apartment complex.

Concrete must be laid first to provide solid foundations for the apartments to be built on. Think of beliefs, relationships and experiences as the concrete. But concrete can't lay itself just as your web cannot weave itself.

Plenty of groundwork is needed to prepare for foundations to be laid. This takes workers, equipment and machinery, all of which are required to build the rest of the complex as well. Think of history, environment and childhood as these three vital elements. They are the mechanics behind the foundations, and are absolutely essential to the construction of the anchor points in your Web of Life.

Take a moment to think about how the environments, childhoods and histories of one generation influence the relationships, experiences and beliefs of the next. When you were born, your parents' childhoods, environments and histories were woven into the anchor points of your web. So your earliest experiences, relationships and beliefs were largely shaped by what was woven (and tangled) within those elements in your parents' webs.

You may have noticed that the counterpart of each of the three foundational elements are present in the mechanics. So all six of these elements are connected by their strands. As all these elements are tied to their counterpart in your web, each strand enables this generational transmission to take place.

I've waited till now to explain this to you for a few reasons. Firstly, the history element gives new meaning to generational cycles and clarifies our understanding of how they come to be. To truly comprehend your connection to the webs of your parents and grandparents it was necessary to first explore history, as you needed to know how and why parts of their webs are interwoven in yours. But mostly it was because you needed an in-depth introduction into all six of these elements and their strands to grasp their collective power and significance.

Now that you are aware of the mechanics behind the foundations of your Web of Life, we can finally explore the remaining two fundamental elements that are intertwined throughout it all.

Element 6: History

STUFF THAT SHOULD STICK

- Beliefs and history form the time strand of your Web of Life.

- History is embedded into everything - so look at history from the world sphere perspective first and *always* consider its counterpart element... it's crucial to understanding ANYTHING!

- All cycles are a product of history - they may be reflected in us as an exact replica of a past infliction or they could be a watered-down version of it.

- You first existed as a precursor cell in both your parents' bodies while each of your grandmothers were pregnant.

- As easily as you can physically resemble a parent or grandparent, you may also resemble them mentally or emotionally. This phenomenon is referred to as inherited family trauma and the evidence can be found in your everyday language.

- The history, childhood and environments of one generation directly impact the structural foundations (or the three anchor points) of the web's of the next; beliefs, relationships and experiences.

CHAPTER 9

Element 7: Energy

"If you want to find the secrets of the universe, think in terms of energy, frequency and vibration."

- Nikola Tesla

We now know that everything is interconnected through energy, from the various systems in our bodies to the furniture in our homes. Energy permeates every atom in the universe and all things are vibrating at a particular frequency. Previously this idea that everything is energy was only associated with theories from physics, metaphysics and spirituality. But thanks to modern scientists like Neil deGrasse Tyson endorsing it, the idea's been embraced by society and has become a fixture in popular culture.

This omnipresent element is interwoven within each thread in your Web of Life. It's the fundamental force that drives your existence and powers your thoughts, emotions and actions, making it essential to all your cycles. However energy also plays a crucial role in how we experience and navigate the world, and especially in how we interact with others.

Cycles in Action

Have you ever been around someone for such a long time that you believe you know them inside and out? You get along so well and know so much about each other that it feels like nothing could ever rock the boat. Then one day something sparks such a strong reaction from them that you wonder if you ever really knew them at all. You can't escape the energy shift that has taken place, and it makes you start questioning everything; particularly why their response was so extreme to something so minor. Suddenly you're seeing a totally different side of this person, and one that you have no idea how to handle.

Element 7: Energy

We're all familiar with this experience because it happens in every relationship. It doesn't matter who it is or how close you are, this is bound to occur at some point. Now as difficult as these experiences are for anyone present (especially for them), the truth is it's necessary. What it is meant to do is to bring their attention to something from their past that's still bugging them.

The experience gives them an opportunity to feel the bug that's tangled in their web and notice *how* they spiral around it. In other words, it's a chance to recognise the unhealed wound that was triggered so they can reflect on the core of the problem, not what it was that bothered them at the time. But if this cannot be accomplished they can still discover something about themselves, as how they react emotionally, mentally and physically shows them a cycle within their Web of Life.

Have you ever thought a bug was dead and only realised it wasn't when you tried to pick it up? As soon as you touched it you knew it was alive because it started to wiggle. It may be a strange coincidence, but this accurately describes what's happening here too. Except the wiggling is replaced with a different yet equally frantic burst of energy, and this one is much harder to squash than a wiggling bug.

Like the bugs that appear dead, the bugs in your web remain still as long as they're undisturbed. So as we weave around the rest of our webs and spiral around other bugs, we may not notice its presence. When you haven't spiralled around one for a while you can forget it exists altogether. But the second it's touched you will come alive with energy as the emotional and mental parts of the cycle start revolving. It doesn't matter if months or years have gone by, if it's still stuck in your web that bug can be always triggered.

We all have cycles that started with an experience that caused us pain or fear on some level, and that needs to be addressed in order to break them. But first we need to know that the cycle exists and the only way to know is for it (and us) to be set off. Now I'm sure we'd all agree that being on the receiving end of a cycle doesn't feel like a projection, therefore what transpires is an infliction of that energy on whoever is present. So until the mystery behind that cycle is revealed, it will keep being repeated as they will be set off by any experience that's connected to that pain or fear.

It's the same as picking on things you don't like in others. The reality is that you dislike the qualities in people that you really don't like in yourself. Your inner self knows the truth of the matter but your outer self has to realise it. The problem is that what you see so clearly in those around you is not so obvious and easy to see *within* you.

So you repeat this cycle and keep inflicting it on others until you realise the truth hidden at its core. This means how long a bug stays stuck in your web is totally up to you. The game is to detangle your web and liberate all your bugs so that you can set *yourself* free. Then you can weave a web of wonder and stop going around in circles. But in order to accomplish this incredible feat you must first face and defeat your toughest opponent - YOU!

Cycles on Repeat

When you are reminded of a previous experience, you're suddenly flooded with emotions from the past. You don't necessarily realise that you've registered the connection, but your subconscious mind joins the dots immediately. In mere seconds the cycle transitions from emotional to mental with uncontrollable thoughts about what's just happened. Although your emotions are heightened and you've barely processed your present experience, on impulse you react and physically expel some of that negative energy out of your body. The more uncomfortable and painful that emotion felt inside you, the more firepower is behind the cycle's infliction onto others; particularly whoever or whatever pushed your buttons.

You may think you have let go of an event from your past, especially when the memory hasn't resurfaced for some time. This could be because you haven't seen the person who bugged you or maybe you haven't been pushed to relive details of that particular event for a while. But a cycle is rarely provoked by an exact replica of the original experience. So it might begin with something that has no apparent tie to the bug at its core, yet the underlying theme is what connects the past with the present. Your job then is to discover what that missing link is, and often the relationship between the two is surprisingly simple.

I can't tell you how many times I believed I was truly over the events I've shared with you, only to find that the slightest hint of that pain brought everything up to the surface. Any critical comment (no matter how small) would take me right back to childhood and the tiniest whiff of betrayal created suspicions in me that were impossible to ignore. When these cycles began I needed to take time away from the situation to reflect on the original bug and simply allow the energy to pass through my body. But I didn't.

Instead I let it go straight to my head and surfed the emotional tidal wave. I didn't mean to inflict that energy on others, but expecting betrayal and being defensive with criticism was how I physically expressed those cycles. So the poor soul who accidentally invoked the memory got sprayed with a few rounds of rapid fire ammo before I had a chance to realise what I had done.

When a cycle is inflicted on you deep down you know it has nothing to do with you. But it's hard to believe this when, in the heat of the moment, all that energy is being directed at you. With no choice but to cop the brunt of it, most people end up taking responsibility for its occurrence and apologise to try to calm the situation.

Though this may appear to be helpful, it's not doing the other person any favours in the long run. To say sorry for making someone's symptoms show isn't solving the *real* problem whatsoever. It actually has the opposite effect (and is an effective strategy on their part). Besides the fact that you're holding *yourself* accountable for *their* actions, you are also enabling them to continue denying the problem is inside of them at all.

You see, when someone repeats a cycle they almost always blame the one who induced it rather than themselves, the one who produced it. The energy of blame is incredibly powerful and can break people easily, which is why you may resort to an apology. But this is a subconscious tactic that keeps the attention off what caused their reaction and allows them to avoid the real issue completely.

Now if you're anything like me and your defence is to go into attack mode, you might make matters worse by adding fuel to the fire instead of apologising. I'm embarrassed to admit it but before I understood what was really going on, I'd launch a few mouth missiles right back at them. When people are reacting they're not quick to become receptive, so it always escalated the situation.

Although it makes sense to want to defend yourself when you feel like you're being attacked, this creates a battle between the two of you when the only battle should be within themselves. At this point in the cycle they actually need your understanding more than they need a reality check. The problem is that we are so deeply affected by the drastic change in energy that we forget to show compassion to the person who caused the shift. But you do them an injustice when you don't support them through this experience, no matter how hostile they may appear at the time.

Rather than apologise or respond to their physical expression (regardless of what form it takes), you're both better off if you get them to trace the cycle back to its beginnings so you can try to uncover the original bug with them. Clearly this must take place when they're calm and coherent, which will only occur once they have finished expressing the cycle and expelling all that energy.

Energy in Motion

The word 'emotion' originates from the Latin word *emovere*, which means 'to move out'. So the energy of your emotions seek *to move out* of your body. Usually they don't move far enough, though, as they get trapped in our minds and are fed with mental energy until they are physically acted upon.

When energy flows through water we see ripples and waves, but technically only the energy is moving, not the water. Water particles simply lift up and down as energy passes through it before returning to its normal state of stillness. It's possible for your emotional energy to flow through you the same way; it just doesn't happen as easily, which is ironic because human beings are roughly 60% water.

If you view your emotions as energy moving out of the body, you can actually feel the waves or ripples as they come up and fade away. Without consciously trying to experience this, however, what happens is your thoughts immediately catch and surf those waves, then get carried away by the current. Emotions get a boost as soon as mental energy is added to the equation because we begin to attach meaning and stories to it.

Perhaps you remind yourself of all the other times something similar happened to you or convince yourself that the experience proved that someone doesn't like you. So what started as a ripple turns into a wave and quickly becomes a gnarly beast. Then before you know it, you are drowning in a sea of self-created negativity.

As an emotion passes through the body it affects your mental state. There's no avoiding it. But the emotion can be fleeting or lasting and it all depends on how much energy you choose to feed it. The problem is your thoughts instantly bind to the emotion of an experience, moving it straight to the mind where your thoughts take over. This is when the stories and meaning making begins, which appears to serve an important purpose at the time but really doesn't serve you at all. The reality is that an emotion can only remain inside your body if you mentally focus on it, otherwise it will naturally fall away on its own.

The crazy thing is this happens all the time when positive events occur in your life. We only seem to feed mental energy to negative experiences. When amazing things happen the emotions are hardly given a second thought so they disappear quite quickly.

Say someone randomly complimented you this morning and made your day or you screamed 'yes!' when you scored the last parking spot at the shops after work. In that moment you felt a powerful (albeit brief) wave of positive emotion. But ten minutes later it's like it never happened. You aren't really thinking about it at all and a day later you've completely forgotten about it.

How different would it be had you been criticised this morning and cut off from the last parking spot instead? Chances are the whole day would've been spent thinking about that comment and anyone you spoke to that night would be told the story about you being cut off. A day later those same events have likely been fed so much energy that the emotions are just as raw but twice as strong as when they first arose.

We do this constantly with negative events from the past and lower our vibrations, so why not do the exact opposite? You have the power to do this at any time, so choose to raise your vibrations whenever you're feeling down. It benefits your mental state when you intentionally put yourself in a positive emotional state.

You can relive a past experience and replicate that ripple of good feeling tones inside you, which sends a surge of positive sensation throughout your entire body. If you feed it more energy and think about all the tiny details of that experience, your thoughts will make the emotion grow stronger and you will feel good for longer. This is the very essence of a daily gratitude journal and it not only heightens your emotional state, but creates a flow on effect in other areas of your life too.

Energy Cycles

The energy of your spirit is eternal, but your mental, emotional and physical energy needs to be replenished daily. I'm sure you're aware that what you consume and surround yourself with impacts your energy levels and overall state of being. When your choices result in your energy being drained rather than nourished then you're stuck in a cycle of depletion. Depression and anxiety reside in this element as they impact energy levels and are cyclical in nature.

There are various sources that deplete your life-force energy and both the quality and quantity of these sources are factored in, so this cycle can take a few different forms. The most common expressions of this cycle are addictions to social media, gaming, pornography and streaming services. We know the importance of making healthy decisions when it comes to foods and beverages, but we forget to apply the same filter to our content choices. What you read, play, watch and listen to should be vetted with the same vigour as the ingredients listed in the products you purchase.

The stresses of life take a toll on our minds and bodies, which means you need to gravitate towards practices that ground, restore, centre and balance your energy. This means spending more time doing activities like yoga, qigong, meditation, ice baths or journalling each day over video games, Netflix, Instagram and TikTok. When you repeatedly sacrifice the essentials of life (like good food, sleep and authentic human connection) for a few more episodes, games or scrolls you're in a cycle of depletion.

It is not just a physical phenomenon as emotional and mental energy is expended or renewed depending on how you manage and direct your attention. Your energy affects those around you and you are similarly impacted by the energy of others. Maybe you've noticed that being in the presence of certain people increases your vitality, makes you happy and uplifts you, while being around others just exhausts you and drags you down. It's not necessarily intentional, some people just give you a boost of energy and others deplete it. That may be part of your cycle.

Take stock of who you're drawn to connect with, who you're not and how you feel after interacting with others. Energy transfers between people in a relationship, so you need to notice how energy is exchanged and recognise any imbalances. As everything is energy this transference takes many forms, so consider if there's equal give and take between you. But remember there will always be people you take energy from too, and that may be the expression of your cycle of depletion.

STUFF THAT SHOULD STICK

- When something or someone bugs you (emotionally, mentally or physically) your job is not to react or respond, but to investigate internally. The same goes for others, so keep that front of mind and don't take things personally.

- **Emotional energy + mental energy = meaning making and story-telling**

- We don't feed energy to the wins and positive events that occur in our daily lives (we just carry on), but we do this for experiences we perceive as negative or the losses (till the cows come home).

- Emotions are energies in motion - you are the one who chooses to let them flow through you and move out of the body or feed them with mental attention and trap that energy inside you. This also happens if you repress or suppress them.

CHAPTER 10

Element 8: Science

It may seem odd that this is a fundamental element in your Web of Life. I must admit that for years I believed there was something more appropriate and applicable that must've just escaped my mind. Yet I kept coming back to the fact that what we consider knowledge is indeed what science has proven and that modern technology wouldn't exist without it.

We now have the luxury of answers at our fingertips, so whenever we want to know or understand anything we can just jump online and science provides us with an explanation. Clearly this element can give you valuable insight into your Web of Life as it contains our collective understanding of everything in the known universe. Although science represents the wealth of information readily available to us, this element specifically relates to *your* personal knowledge, comprehension and application of it.

The Power Strand

There are many powerful connections between science and energy so these two fundamental elements form the power strand of your Web of Life. There is clearly a source of power that gives everything its energy and science is our method of attempting to uncover the truth behind it all.

So energy underlies our understanding of the physical world and science explains the natural processes that govern it. However we are not just physical beings nor do we experience energy exclusively in a physical manner. We also experience powerful energy generated by the thoughts and emotions of ourselves and others. Therefore the power strand is embedded into all your cycles and is fundamental in understanding the other six elements in the Web of Life.

Element 8: Science

Breaking Cycles in Science

Funnily enough not even this element is exempt from being stuck in cycles just like the rest of us. In actuality, since its beginnings belief cycles have plagued science, which slowed the necessary progression of many disciplines. This meant that many breakthroughs were ignored or completely rejected at first, and sometimes for decades. Other scientists had their work disregarded in their lifetime only to be rediscovered much later. This shows us that the essence of what was deemed science in the past was based more on the time strand (beliefs and history) rather than facts.

Throughout history scientists have been charged with the task of challenging social beliefs, ensuring they were not only pioneers in their respective fields, but in cycle breaking too. Albert Einstein referred to Galileo as 'the father of modern science' for this reason and because he was instrumental in establishing the scientific method. Although he paid a heavy price for going against the Catholic Church, his revolutionary contributions to physics, mathematics, philosophy and astronomy paved the way for all the advancements that followed. Since Galileo countless others have broken similar cycles in the world sphere, though this vital role is not exclusive to scientists.

Everyday people break belief cycles when they defy death sentences or make miraculous recoveries after being diagnosed with a terminal illness or incurable disease. However some individuals draw media attention and spark global movements after achieving something considered scientifically impossible. This proves that anyone can assist in the evolution of science. Just as global events infiltrate our social and self spheres, what starts with one person can spread throughout the planet. This is precisely what happened with the groundbreaking work of the greatest scientists in history and, more recently, the Wim Hofs of the world.

The Dutch extreme athlete also known as "The Iceman" first got his name by breaking nearly 20 world records with his outstanding performance in icy temperatures. He attributed his amazing abilities to the Wim Hof Method®, which combines breathing exercises, mindset or concentration training and gradual cold exposure. Believing him to be an anomaly, scientists started studying him while he practiced his method. Incredibly they found his body temperature remained constant despite being immersed in ice for 80 minutes.[14]

But as he claimed that he could influence his autonomic nervous system, the body's innate immune response, an additional experiment was conducted in 2011. He was injected with components of E. coli bacteria as previous studies had shown it makes the body think it's under attack, which causes the immune system to over-react and flu-like symptoms to emerge.

At the height of the symptoms for the 112 other test subjects, Hof was only experiencing a mild headache, while his body produced less than half the number of inflammatory proteins as they averaged. Basically his body barely reacted and yet the symptoms hardly showed. So it was concluded that his concentration technique enabled him to produce a controlled response to the bacteria, proving that he could influence his autonomic nervous system and his immune response.

As it was still believed that these systems couldn't be influenced he was considered to be an extraordinary case. Wim Hof didn't think he was an anomaly so the study was replicated in 2014 and the same results were produced by the 12 volunteers he'd trained for ten days prior to the experiment.[15] He then began sharing his method with the world and now multiple studies are measuring its effectiveness on the mind and body.

Hof's work has unlocked the hidden potential of our biology and unleashed a wealth of new knowledge that overturns 150 years of scientific thinking. We are not nearly as limited as science has led us to believe, and these kinds of discoveries often result from individual's breaking cycles in science. So using the three spheres approach we will now explore some cycles in this element that directly affect your web.

The World Sphere

This perspective considers the world's scientific knowledge and understanding from the time you were born up until now. This includes advances in technology and how available or accessible they were. Prior to the internet, what information was able to reach you and your social sphere depended on how effectively it was disseminated around the world. We had only television, books and newspapers to keep us informed and tell us what we needed to know.

Now we are bombarded with information from a myriad of sources, yet the truth is more elusive than ever! We are immersed in so much misinformation it's a full-time job to discern fact from fiction. This has significant implications for science, as important information often gets drowned out by the latest gossip about celebrities or social media influencers. It's therefore vital to go to reputable sources and renowned scientists to improve your own knowledge.

In the first episode of his show Missing Links, host and scientist Gregg Braden identifies the three global cycles that are responsible for the extremes we are currently experiencing. These conflict, economic and climate cycles occur naturally and each have their own rhythms, which are so precise that they can actually be calculated. But for the first time in history all three collided in 2017.[16]

The economic cycle isn't just about money, but also concerns people working together and sharing vital resources such as food and medicine around the world. It is characterised by four distinct phases of inflation, also known as the Kondratieff seasons, with each season occurring for approximately 15-20 years. Since roughly 2000 we've been in the winter, or deflation phase, distinguished by high unemployment rates and banking crises.

The conflict cycle begins with conditions that cause tensions to rise in societies, nations and world regions. This makes humanity more prone to events like wars and riots, which consequently serve as a catalyst for major social change. The cycle occurs around every 18 years and the peaks coincide with the height of every war or serious conflict we've ever had on Earth. Meanwhile the troughs always align with the endings of these battles.

The current cycle began its uptick in 2014 and peaked in the year 2020, so we were more susceptible to conflict during this time.[17] Given it was the year of the global pandemic and mass lockdowns you'd think that human conflict would've been forcibly contained. That couldn't be further from the truth. We saw a surge in worldwide unrest, riots and protests, and 2020 will go down in history due to the overwhelming global demonstrations in support of the Black Lives Matter movement.

Scientists can gather information about Earth's climate from ancient tree rings, core samples taken from beneath the sea floor and the ice sheets of Antarctica and Greenland. Data collected from these sources show 420,000 years of climate history on our planet and have found that the temperature of Earth repeatedly cools and warms over time. We are currently in the warming period of the cycle, which is why we are experiencing above normal temperatures around the globe.

Element 8: Science

Now climate change and global warming have been heavily debated for some time, yet the data doesn't support what we've been told. Rising levels of greenhouse gases are not causing temperatures to rise. Warming periods are always brief but intense and are followed by rapid cooling. This is what causes levels of greenhouse gases in the atmosphere to increase, particularly carbon dioxide. The cycle also has a gap of between 400-700 years from the time the temperature increases to when the gas levels rise.[18]

So why does any of this matter to you? Well first of all, these cycles provide fascinating evidence in support of the notion that history repeats itself. It's instructive to be aware of the rhythm of these cycles as there are implications for your life. Knowing what's on the global horizon can help you better manage your finances, and being aware of peak periods of hostility can encourage more peaceful resolutions to conflicts.

Now you know how differently data can be interpreted when there are agendas and incentives involved. This is not to say that science is corrupt, but that there are variables that influence how and what information is presented. It's therefore wise to consult peer-reviewed sources to clarify your own understanding rather than relying on quick Google searches for the latest and most accurate information.

The Social Sphere

In Chapter 8 you learned that trauma in your family history is woven into your web. You also learned that your inception dates back five months into your grandmother's pregnancy when she was carrying your mother. Emerging research can explain how this connection enables the residue of trauma to be inherited, however there is a little more to this story that I've waited till now to tell you.

It's well known that a mother's stress while pregnant can affect her child. Her emotions release hormones and information signals into her bloodstream, which also transfers vital nutrients to the foetus in her womb. This causes a series of behavioural, metabolic and physiological changes that are mirrored in the mother and her unborn child.[19] When pregnant mothers experience constant or extreme stress those children will inherit stress patterns from their mother.

After contemplating the information that follows, I'm certain you will regard the above inheritance as the most basic and simple level possible. The true scope with which you can be impacted by the experiences of family members is, as you will now discover, far more extensive and interesting.

Your father's sperm was susceptible to traumatic imprints almost until the moment of your conception as it continued to multiply when he reached puberty and developed all throughout adulthood. On the other hand your mother's egg cells formed whilst she was in her mother's womb, at which point that cell line stopped dividing. Then she was born with her lifelong supply of eggs and regardless of how many years passed, you developed from one of them after it was fertilised by your father's sperm.[20]

Now this is where it gets crazy. Not only was this egg (you) able to be imprinted by your mother's traumas, but the precursor cell to the egg from which you developed was able to be imprinted from traumas your grandmother experienced whilst she was pregnant with your mother. Although your existence was purely on a cellular level at this time, as your mother and grandmother shared the same biological environment this made you vulnerable to this inheritance.[21] This is another important reason why you should know the family traumas woven into the history element of your web.

Element 8: Science

You might recall that Wolynn found the cycle of trauma surfacing through the everyday language of patients just like Gretchen. But scientists can actually identify evidence of this transference through biological markers. Rachel Yehuda is a renowned neuroscientist, researcher and professor recognised for her pioneering work on post-traumatic stress disorder (PTSD) and, more recently, the intergenerational transmission of trauma. She was among the first researchers to demonstrate how descendants could exhibit physical and emotional symptoms of traumas they didn't personally experience.[22]

Yehuda looked at the neurobiology of PTSD in Holocaust survivors, war veterans and women who were pregnant during 9/11. She discovered that levels of cortisol, the body's stress hormone, were low in PTSD. This was controversial as it challenged historical beliefs that high levels were associated with stress. What was more surprising, however, was that the same results were mirrored in their children.[23]

Children of Holocaust survivors who had PTSD were actually born with low levels of cortisol, making them susceptible to reliving their parents symptoms. Therefore low levels are the biomarker that indicates trauma has been passed down. Although this was disputed at first, her research ultimately provided the clarity needed to transform our understanding and treatment of PTSD.

Remarkably, Yehuda discovered that cortisol ends the stress response by signalling safety after the event has occurred, which allows the body to rebalance itself naturally. However these hormones don't return to equilibrium in PTSD, so the stress response continues in the body long after the danger has passed.[24]

In light of these findings, her research concluded that if our parents had PTSD then we are three times more likely to experience the same symptoms, and it's also likely we'll suffer from anxiety or depression.[25] Given how common depression and anxiety is amongst today's youth, I can't help but think the intergenerational transmission of trauma provides an explanation for the startling numbers we see.

The Self Sphere

As several fields study the complex inner and outer worlds of our species, all the elements and strands in your web have disciplines specifically dedicated to their exploration. Though the self sphere takes into account your level of comprehension as a whole, it mainly relates to your knowledge of information directly connected to you. So a good jumping off point would be to reflect on your understanding of the science behind each of the elements, however right now it's important to contemplate the information presented in this chapter as there are obvious implications for your web and for your life.

As a matter of fact, now in psychotherapy it's not unusual for traumatic events in an individual's family and social history to be considered alongside their personal traumas to gain a more comprehensive understanding of a person.[26] So as difficult as it might be, it's necessary to explore the big and little ts in your own family, especially knowing that they aren't just interwoven in your web but could very well be imprinted *in* you.

These studies were based on survivors of major world events, so you might be thinking that your parents or grandparents never experienced anything as severe. This doesn't have any bearing on whether or not they developed PTSD during their lifetime, but let's just say they didn't - does that somehow diminish the effects that can result even from little ts?

Element 8: Science

Of course not.

Though the social sphere delved into the science behind intergenerational transmission, we cannot lose sight of the fact that the cycle of trauma is also inflicted. The saying 'hurt people, hurt people' exists for a reason. It's rare for anyone to go through life without adversity and the consequences can be catastrophic.

Research has found that chronic neglect and emotional abuse can have the same effects as physical abuse or sexual molestation.[27] Besides, anything emotionally disturbing can be traumatic and it doesn't need to be first-hand experience either. Nor is trauma limited to childhood experiences. So there's plenty for you to consider.

Science helps us make sense of everything in our world, including ourselves, and explains the hows and whys of all natural phenomenon. Though a lot depends on your interests and, quite frankly, how technologically literate you are, there is a lot of value to be gained from self-education. Keeping up with advancements in science and technology would be virtually impossible as new discoveries and debates emerge daily. But there are obvious benefits to being informed and many practical applications for your life, most notably to improve your health, wealth, relationships and decision-making.

> "Nothing has such power to broaden the mind as the ability to investigate systematically and truly all that comes under thy observation in life."
>
> - Marcus Aurelius

STUFF THAT SHOULD STICK

- Energy and science form the power strand of your Web of Life. This strand is the essence of the entire web, so both elements run through all six others and every single cycle - that's why it's called the power strand!

- Science has been breaking cycles since its beginnings and people doing this is *vital* to evolve our understanding of ourselves, our consciousness and our universe. Breaking cycles on the personal, societal and global fronts also makes for a more positive planetary experience for us all, don't you think?

- The whole world is impacted by climate, conflict and economic cycles each with different revolutions - *all* of which hit the planet simultaneously for the first time in 2017. And aren't we still reeling from this first global historical cycle in 2023?

- Being a precursor cell in the bodies of both parents while in the womb made you susceptible to being imprinted by traumas experienced by your grandmother - so it's *critical* to explore the possibilities for the intergenerational transmission of trauma in your family heritage (and consider its implications for your web *as a whole*!)

CHAPTER 11

It's All Connected

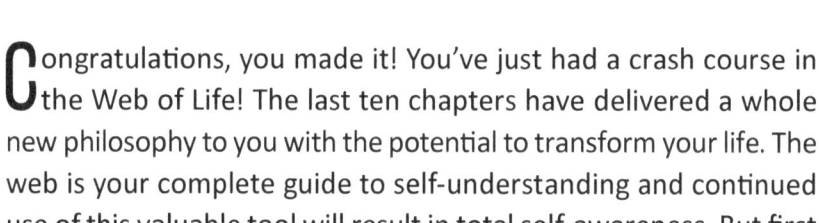

Congratulations, you made it! You've just had a crash course in the Web of Life! The last ten chapters have delivered a whole new philosophy to you with the potential to transform your life. The web is your complete guide to self-understanding and continued use of this valuable tool will result in total self-awareness. But first you have to remember it all.

Once I started introducing it to people I found it challenging to recall all of the eight fundamental elements and their strands. To make it simple and easy for you I have an acronym that helps you memorise the elements. It follows the same sequence with which they were introduced to you.

Beliefs
Relationships
Experiences
Environment
Childhood
History
Energy
Science

The acronym is BREECHES. Instantly I think of breech births, when the baby comes out the wrong and extra painful way. That's a little trick to remember the fundamental elements and what happens when you spiral around the bugs stuck in them. A negative cycle breeches your life-force energy by keeping you going around in circles, which stops you from weaving around your web with ease and flow.

In case you're not the type of person who naturally learns information presented this way, I have an alternate method that you might prefer:

The Elements

Beliefs + Relationships = Experiences
Environment + Childhood = History
Energy + Science = EVERYTHING!

The Strands

Beliefs + History = Time Strand
Relationships + Environment = Foundation Strand
Childhood + Experiences = Super Strand
Science + Energy = Power Strand

Using the mathematics trick for the elements I was able to remember that the foundations of the web is the first sum, the second sum are the mechanics behind the foundations, and the last sum is woven through everything. But I got confused sometimes as there are three elements that start with the letter e. So this sentence helped me remember their order: **Our experiences are influenced by our environment and the energy around us.**

The best thing to do is to have the Web of Life PDF somewhere you see a lot so you become familiar with it. I always have a printed copy on my fridge so it stays fresh in my mind. I put it on a mug so I saw it multiple times a day (you can get one on my website) and it was the screensaver on my phone for a while too. Having the web close by helped me take myself out of whatever I was going through and go within to work out what was really going on. That's how you detangle your Web of Life!

Facing the Mirror

There are many opportunities for connection in the world yet we feel so isolated from others and are disconnected from ourselves. What we choose to occupy our time with just keeps us distracted and stops us from turning our focus internally. This isn't an accident, though. It happens on purpose.

We avoid going within, because we are afraid of confronting the negative aspects of ourselves. You may have heard the term *shadow* referring to this darker side we all possess. But we don't want to see it or know about it and when someone else points it out to us we reject it. Why are we so desperate to avoid the very thing that will liberate us so can we live a life of happiness and freedom?

Well, it's not easy to face harsh truths about ourselves, so our natural instinct is to ignore them whenever they're brought to our attention. They're not pretty and don't make us feel warm and fuzzy, so if we refuse to acknowledge their existence we don't have to deal with them. It's confronting to accept the ugly things we've done, the ugly parts of our personalities, our ugly past experiences and our ugly methods of coping with it all. Not to mention that becoming aware of our issues, learning where they came from and healing them is a long and lonely road. But it doesn't have to be.

It's definitely easier to stay in our comfort zones where there are no challenges, but growth only happens when you dare to do things differently. Looking in the proverbial mirror is your answer and the Web of Life is your cheat sheet. It will help you achieve the future that you envision and embody the best version of yourself. Detangling your web will strip you of your self-imposed limitations so you can love life and yourself *unconditionally*. If you embrace the process you can soar through this journey and upscale your life.

The Web of Life is your guide to complete self-discovery, recovery and mastery. Discovery means learning to identify your cycles, understanding how they work and recognising them in action. Recovery begins when you start tending to what needs to be healed or worked through and improving your experience of life. Mastery is accomplished when you're breaking your cycles and freeing the bugs in your web.

So now that you grasp the promising journey behind this philosophy, I can reveal some practical ways for you to get cracking on it.

The Passive Spectator and the Expert Witness

You know that everything happens inside you before anything is expressed on the outside for others to see. So we spend most of our time thinking and feeling. Thoughts and feelings run constantly and repeat against our will like they're programmed (which they are), and this goes on even when no action is being taken. In order to break every other cycle, first you have to learn to break this one.

The start of a cycle is felt in your body as a rising emotion or heard in your mind as a strong thought. However it begins the cycle is quickly joined by the other form, and it happens so fast that you believe they're both occurring at the same time. The energy of this connection feels so big and powerful that you immediately want to expel it. So you do. A cycle ends by being expressed in physical form, through words, actions or inaction. Then we regret how we've responded to the people or events in our lives, without ever inquiring within to uncover how and why we did it in the first place.

This stops now.

Try to catch yourself feeding mental energy to your emotions, or emotional energy to your thoughts. It *will* happen without you realising and that's ok. You're human. It takes time, focus and energy to discover your inner workings, but the good news is that cycles will reveal themselves naturally so just keep on being you. All you need to do is shine the spotlight on them as they pop up and watch how they unfold with curiosity. Your end goal is to get to the point where you are completely aware you're repeating a cycle *while you're doing it* and engage in the whole process consciously.

So your initial goal is to become a passive spectator and then graduate to an expert witness. When you're alert to your inner workings and discovering how a cycle functions you are being a passive spectator. When you can explain a complete cycle to yourself or to others then you have become the expert witness. So after you become aware of a cycle the first step is to learn how it functions.

You know when you wake up and you're left with impressions of a crazy dream you had? You have details in pieces but the sequence doesn't make any sense. All you're left with are vague bits of events that are so disjointed you can't explain them properly. When you unconsciously repeat a cycle that's exactly what it's like. Being a passive spectator enables you to recall every detail of the dream and when you have the power to wake up inside of it you've become the expert witness.

Ever heard Eckhart Tolle say "be the observer, not the participant"? What he's saying is to be a passive spectator watching the amazing show that is you in action. After you've seen yourself in the same performance a few times you start to learn your lines and moves, right? Well when you can witness a cycle in motion rather than just participating in it you have become the expert.

He also says to "be with what is" which is great advice, but it doesn't really help people resolve what goes on inside the mind and body. We want to know what to do with all that energy swirling around inside of us while things outside are bugging us. Letting it pass sounds simple but goes against our natural inclinations. It's much easier said than done. So instead we get overwhelmed and overstimulated by our own energy and end up repeating our cycles, then feel guilty that we couldn't just let it pass.

Remaining aware and present when you're triggered allows you to notice what occurs mentally and emotionally, but then what?

It's All Connected

Yes, you allowed yourself to think and feel and no, you didn't react or respond outwardly. However you're still carrying that energy inside you with no clue how to channel it. A passive spectator takes notes on what's occurring inside them at this point. So you're still expressing the cycle physically, but in a new and improved form that secures your future success.

Truth be told for a while you will only realise you've repeated a cycle *after* you have done it. That's okay. Don't feel down on yourself because this is a normal part of the journey. It's like if you promised yourself today that you'd never swear again. What would happen? You would only realise you've sworn just after you've done it, right? But this makes you notice what thoughts and emotions arise *before* you swear. Once you've revealed the subtle hints you missed last time you start to look out for them. That's the point.

So after you realise a cycle's been expressed, just work backwards and figure out how it happened. Basically you reverse-engineer the cycle by remembering what you felt and thought to make it physical. Knowing the inner signs and signals teaches you to recognise when it's likely to happen again so you can be aware as it unfolds next time.

WARNING!

Immediately after becoming aware of a cycle you will feel compelled to break it. Don't do it! Don't stop the cycle being expressed! It's a trap! I made that mistake for years so I know for a fact that it's nothing but a setback.

When you focus only on stopping what you physically do you are going the wrong (and long) way around breaking cycles. It lets the inner parts escape your awareness which means you'll be constantly fighting back urges to do the physical things you stopped, even when you haven't expressed the cycle that way in months. Take it from me, knowing the mental and emotional parts of a cycle *is* the game-changer!

Being the passive spectator teaches you that the inner cycles are your alert system. With practice you improve your awareness, but in the process you discover how to hack *into* this system. Putting the spotlight on negative thoughts and emotions takes away their power which gives you control over the start of the cycle. Now you've graduated to the expert witness and can participate in it consciously. This exclusive position allows you to obtain the last pieces of useful information needed to complete your cycle-breaking starter kit.

Detangling your Web

Our environments and our relationships will keep creating experiences that bug us. Though at the time it seems like the worst thing happening to you, in truth it's actually a good thing happening *for* you. If you react your emotions are not being felt or processed in the moment, you're just releasing that burst of energy inside you. Rather than lose yourself to this powerful current, from now on follow it and turn these unavoidable ordeals into wins for your future self.

Next time you're bugged by something or someone, notice the emotion emerging and feel the sensations in your body. Ask yourself what emotion it is. It sounds odd, but telling yourself "this is a negative emotional cycle" disrupts the impulse you have to act upon it. More importantly, it slows the connection to a mental cycle so you can work out what your body is trying to tell you.

Be mindful that emotions are surprisingly easy to mislabel. For example we often confuse hurt, sadness, fear and frustration with anger. So to avoid making this mistake take note of the emotion and describe the sensations you feel so next time you can immediately recognise that the cycle is starting to repeat again.

I'm not going to lie, as soon as emotions arise your mind starts to think. It's a mammoth task to stop your emotions marching off with your thoughts because they fall in line like soldiers. This is why we tend to miss the point where these cycles connect, and they bind together so quickly we mistakenly believe they occurred simultaneously.

But the moment you realise it's happening, stop feeding any more energy to your thoughts and tell yourself "this is a negative mental cycle". Try to recall your initial thought and note it. The longer you take to notice your mind was carried off by the emotional current, the further away your mind was taken by the waves of negative energy. This will result in a series of thoughts you'll need a record of.

It's incredibly challenging, but do your best not to get swept up into the sea of emotion that makes you start thinking into how you feel. This impels you to respond, react, forecast future actions or concoct stories about the experience. Feeding the mental cycle any energy is only fuelling it, which you won't realise until it's too late and you're aching for it to get physical.

Now you may appear to be glitching in front of whoever or whatever bugged you in the first place, but who cares? Your introspection and reflection is necessary at this time, not your reaction or response to the catalyst. If your continued presence will only escalate the matter then take inspired action. If it's a person, tell them you have better things to do with your time (which clearly you do) and walk away. If it's a work situation or something similar, haul your ass outta there or simply find another space where you can do the prep work needed to break this cycle.

Keep in mind that reacting or responding when you're bugged by someone isn't the end of the world. You need to know all the ways this cycle manifests, don't you? It's ok if you launch mouth missiles, storm off, mastermind a smear campaign, shut down, give them the cold shoulder or plot a full-scale counter attack.

All you need to do is note exactly how you expressed it afterwards (and maybe apologise). So even losing your composure is proven to be useful. It's a win-win no matter what happens! If at the time you're not in a position (or the mood) to self-inquire about the inner workings of the cycle, there's some good news. You can skip it for now and do some important recon work on the bug instead.

The same way you cover the wound to protect it when you are injured, when you are hurt by an experience you wrap around the bug so you can protect yourself. Then you weave around other elements in your web to keep it secure, and these elements are connected to the cycle you created. From then on whenever you detect a similar experience, you try to shield yourself from feeling that hurt again by either repeating the cycle or reacting like the past event is happening now. So that person, place or situation isn't *really* what's bugging you, it's what remains unresolved. Your goal is to reveal it and heal it.

It's hardly a mystery; the link to the past usually registers inside us. So strongly, in fact, that we'll often announce it as part of the physical expression of our cycle. Connecting a past experience to your present one means you've identified the bug. Basically it's a defence strategy - revealing the bug explains *why* we're spiralling.

For instance, take someone who was cheated on in a previous relationship stressing over unanswered calls and texts. When they speak to their partner they'll likely react from the place of hurt and tell their partner that it's because they were being cheated on last time this happened to them. We often reveal the bug (core wound) as part of our reaction because it explains that we felt the same pain again, which explains why we repeated the cycle.

This is when you bring yourself back to the Web of Life and consider how it's attached to the fundamental elements. Then you will understand why you repeat the same cycle in response to circumstances that appear totally separate from each another; what they have in common *is* the bug. Once you know its origin, the element it's stuck in and how you spiral around it, you can detangle this knot in your Web of Life!

Then the next time you're similarly bugged as opposed to getting lost in your emotional and mental cycles you'll start to follow them like leads. Rather than completing the cycle, you will consciously witness what you're thinking, feeling and about to say or do *as* you're doing it. Now you have achieved the supreme status of expert and are ready to break the cycle.

The reason you keep going around in circles is because of past experiences. Spiralling around that bug keeps the past alive so the pain remains as raw as when it was first felt. Freeing the bug from your web allows you to free yourself from holding onto the pain and the past. By releasing your attachment to the core experience you transmute that negative energy you still carry within you. The more profound result that comes from breaking a cycle, however, is forgiveness; first of the self and then of others.

STUFF THAT SHOULD STICK

🕸 The acronym BREECHES = beliefs, relationships, experiences, environment, childhood, history, energy, science. Write it down and stick it somewhere to absorb the elements of the web.

🕸 3 e's trick to remember their order - **experiences are influenced by our environments and energy.** Helpful hint - write it down somewhere you see frequently to guide your awareness of this fact throughout your experiences. If your mind thinks differently try **experiences = environment + energy**.

🕸 You're the passive spectator when you're learning how your cycles operate by being aware and present *as* you repeat them.

🕸 You've stepped up your game and reached the supreme status of expert witness when you know the ins and outs of a cycle and how you operate within it (what you feel, think and do/not do). Once there, you're now ready to expand your consciousness and master the self as you BREAK THE CYCLE!!!

CHAPTER 12

It's Time to Break the Cycle

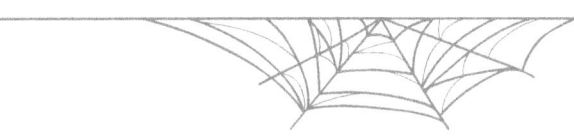

Here comes the life-changing secret you've been waiting for! You already know about the 4mation of a cycle, so now I can reveal the simple formula you can use to break them all! The best part is that the same 4 phases that make a cycle actually holds the secret to breaking them. The only difference is the entire process is in reverse!

Believe it or not, this was the last piece of my Web of Life puzzle... and it took me almost 3 years to find it! I'd been looking at the 4mation of a cycle everyday without realising the answer was right in front of me the whole time! If only I'd known I wouldn't have wasted years of my life trying to figure out how to do it through a painstaking process of research and experimentation.

One night I was staring longingly at the 4mation poster on the wall. I was so tired of trying different strategies and getting nowhere, and just wished I could break cycles as easily as I created them. I was looking at the word expression when it suddenly dawned on me that all these things people were doing, the positive affirmations, rewriting stories, visualisations, gratitude journals and vision boards... they're all just different forms of *expression!*

Immediately I wondered what would happen if I drew the 4mation ring in reverse. The second I saw it my inner knowing burst with excitement because it made *total* sense. This breakthrough was truly mind-blowing! Breaking cycles was no longer a mystery and the Web of Life was finally complete. Instantly I realised that I'd created a practical, comprehensive and powerful formula for self-discovery, recovery and mastery that the world needed just as much as I did!

So let's get into the 4 phases of breaking a cycle.

Expression

When you're about to do something new and different in your life like start a business, quit smoking or travel to another country, what's the first thing you do? You tell someone, right? Expressing our intention turns a possibility into a probability. It's how we put our dreams and desires out into the universe and affirm with certainty that we're going to make it happen.

Announcing that you're breaking a cycle is exciting. Your goal will always be approved by anyone you tell and chances are you'll inspire them to transform their lives as well. But don't just share the old cycle you're breaking - tell them about the positive one you're replacing it with! Verbalise what you're leaving behind and forecast how your life will change.

When people want to manifest something into their lives they start by feeling the emotions of having achieved it. The book *The Secret* got people living as though their life was already exactly how they desired. That's the idea here. Expression encourages you to let go of the past cycle and bring forth the future one. This is the key to unlock your personal power and freedom!

Now you've probably noticed that this is not the same as expression when making a cycle. When cycles are made (or repeated), expression is what comes out as a result of what's gone on inside of you. *If* you realise what you said or did it'll only happen afterwards.

Expression when you break a cycle is a complete reversal of this process. What comes out of you and everything you surround yourself with expresses the future change you envision for your inner and outer worlds. This is done consciously and intentionally. By using multiple methods of expression you will push yourself to accomplish your goal and break the cycle.

Look, no one is eager to face challenges head on and take bold, new actions when you're uncertain of the outcome. Stepping into unfamiliar territory is overwhelming, and it's scary to let go and move forward when the road ahead is unknown. That's why the saying is the devil you know, right? Hell, it took me 5 years to take the leap and share the Web of Life with the world!

You see, I know fear well. It held me captive in my comfort zone when I knew I needed to break free of things in my life - relationships, jobs, lifestyles. It didn't matter how much I wanted change, my hesitation was killing my motivation. So the benefit of expression is that it mentally and emotionally prepares you. You set yourself up for success before the challenge really sets in by boosting your spirit and energising your willpower.

You do this by feeding as much energy to the emerging cycle as possible. How do you do that? Well, the more kinds of expression you use, the more positive your cycle-breaking journey will be!

The most important thing to remember is you are fuelling your momentum. The more ways you can express your goal and the more often you do it, the closer that information is to being integrated inside you to become knowledge. That's the purpose behind the expression phase.

So be innovative with the things you like to do and use them in as many different ways as you can imagine. If you draw, paint, dance, write and sing for example, then incorporate combinations of these into your everyday life. But keep them focused on your cycle-breaking. It's important to use types of expression that are authentic to you, so it's easy and fun! The more you're cramming into your life, the more prepared you are for the next phase.

Music is by far the most potent tool you can use. It's incredibly versatile and its power is undeniable, not to mention it happens at the press of a button. Be creative with it and breaking the cycle can be a blast!

In the same way you listen to music that connects to your life experiences, emotions and thoughts - you can choose songs that inspire, motivate, uplift you and relate to your goal. You need to create an insatiable desire to break the cycle and experience the new one in your life. Music is a fun way to do it and its potential use is only as limited as your imagination!

To break the cycle of unworthiness I had to whole-heartedly believe in myself. It was the only way to have the confidence I needed to write this book and share the Web of Life with the world. There is no room for self-doubt with a goal *that* big.

So I did an audit on the music I listened to and became obsessed with anything that expressed my new belief cycle. I played songs like 'Girl on Fire' by Alicia Keys, 'Thunder' by Imagine Dragons and 'Champion' by Carrie Underwood (featuring Ludacris) on repeat. I would fall asleep hearing frequencies for self-love, manifestation and success.

But I didn't just listen. I sang. I danced. I remixed the lyrics to make them my own. I replaced any words I could with Ally. I wrote the songs out as poems in my phone and decorated them with emojis. I'd have them playing in the background while I did housework, got ready and whenever I was driving. I'd play them while I was writing in my gratitude journal about successfully breaking the cycle. I lived and breathed these songs until I felt like they were mine. But that's not all I did!

Positive affirmations are an effective tool to rewrite the inner parts of most cycles. I didn't just write them on paper though. I wrote them on my mirror and read it aloud when I walked past it. I'd write it on my shower screens and windows when they fogged up. I recorded myself saying them and listened to it while walking in nature. I even sang them in the car while it was warming up.

I made vision boards of my life before, during and after breaking the cycle, but they weren't always physical. It's not that I couldn't have images and words to represent all parts of the cycle of unworthiness, I just didn't want to feed it the same level of energy as the during and after ones. But you can definitely benefit from doing it, so don't let me stop you!

I'd imagine what it was like to live free of that cycle, then I would digitally create a scene using apps like Procreate. This brought that experience to life so I could look at the image and instantly tap back into the emotions of that visualisation. I'd use it to record a voice memo of a day living this liberated life. Afterwards I'd look and listen at the same time and watch as my body exploded with so much excitement that I couldn't wait to make it my reality.

Not only did it make the goal more alluring, but it also lit a fire under my butt so I would start integrating the new cycle into my life. Then I'd write a series of journal entries to capture the essence of each phase of my journey. I'm sure you can guess where it started and ended, but the best entries were actually the ones where I wrote about falling back into the old cycle.

I didn't write about giving up and having to start again or being a failure and believing I couldn't do it. I wrote about how the lesson I learned from it helped me master myself. I wrote the entry embodying the attitude I needed to break through the challenges I was going to face so I could fulfil my destiny.

Of all my expressions in this phase, those entries were the ones I kept going back to. In the end, they're also the ones I'm most grateful for because they kept me focused on growth and progress, which is the next phase of the formula.

Integration

When making a cycle, the knowledge you gain from an experience integrates with your thoughts and emotions to form the inner parts. When breaking it, you stop these negative cycles the instant you know they're revolving and integrate the new ones into your life.

It'll always be easier to stick with the old cycle but take it from me, when you start breaking it, it is *electrifying*. It boosts your confidence and makes you feel amazing. But that doesn't guarantee you'll break it every time it appears. And it will keep popping up unexpectedly.

This is a trick that the old cycle plays on you. It'll pop up and run, trying to catch you off guard. It's as if while you're trying to break the cycle, *it* tries to break *you*. So if you're not paying attention to what's going on inside your mind and body, you will miss a shot at integration and just repeat the old cycle.

If the inner parts slip by your awareness remember that the next best thing to breaking a cycle is stopping it from going full circle. You will know the old one has repeated because you'll have the urge to express it physically. That's okay! The integration phase *will* have ups and downs, but all your hard work to get to this point has prepared you for this moment.

You know that to break a cycle you need to notice when it's repeating and stop it *before* it comes out of you. Even if you don't notice until after it's become physical, that's okay. It's actually an important part of the integration phase.

Don't ever think that when you fail to break a cycle, you're doomed. I'm sorry to say it but you are destined to fail… many times. Although you may think you've made absolutely no progress, persevering through this adversity is the key to your success.

It's like when you're meditating and can't empty your mind. Failing to get to the quiet state makes you give up, right? Yet, to keep going *despite* this challenge is how you attain the result and flourish.

Breaking cycles is exactly the same. What you need to know for the new and positive cycles to become your reality comes directly from what you learn when you fail. Like everything in life it's about growth and progress, not perfection. You *will* fail and that's the best part because every time you do, it provides a useful lesson to help you in the future and makes it that little bit easier to overcome the power of the old cycle.

It's Time to Break the Cycle

It's like when someone pays you a compliment. It slides right off and you've usually forgotten about it ten minutes later. Criticism, on the other hand, sticks like glue! Years could go by and not only do you remember exactly what was said, but precisely how you felt in that moment. You can replay it in your mind without having to think because it's resurfaced so easily and so often that you've relived that memory more times than you can count.

Your old cycles are like criticism. Don't waste your time feeding them energy. Just keep going after you fall back into them. Don't dwell on it and feel bad about yourself because it's not worth it. You can't win. You'll lose sight of the future and get stuck in the past.

Trust me, there were times where I'd focus on the mistake so long I missed the lesson. I'd forget I had any success so other old cycles would start to creep in. Before I knew it, I'd spiralled back to bug one and had to start expression all over again to give me a burst of positivity.

You see, although positive energy is stronger at the time it also wears off much faster. Negativity has an energy that lingers which allows it to gain strength over time. So like criticism, it has more staying power. As crazy as it sounds, bring on the bugs is the best attitude to have because being triggered gives you another chance to break the cycle and integrate the new one!

You can't expect to stop what's been revolving for decades in a day, but using the right tools gives you the critical support you need to succeed. You don't break your cycles immediately just like you don't stop a tyre rolling down a hill by standing in its way once. But you do slow it down and if you keep getting ahead of it, eventually it loses momentum and stops. This is why you must continue using your favourite types of expression. That's the trick to help you get in front of negative cycles so you can integrate positive ones in their place.

The purpose of integration is to begin to embody the experiences you will have when the cycle is completely broken. Remember for now the goal is growth, not glory. You are developing your agency so you step into your full power and own it.

As you start integrating the new cycle in your life you really begin to believe that you can break the old one for good. It won't disappear overnight but the more you starve it of energy, attention and repetition over time, the faster the bug dissolves and the cycle fades away.

Knowledge

By the time you're approaching this step, you've already started to break the cycle. But for this phase to be effective, you need to be in a position whereby the old one is consistently being recognised and replaced by the new one, no matter how or when it appears. It won't be without the odd hiccup and that's okay. You just need to have had enough success to genuinely *believe* that you have the power and potential to master these challenges. The purpose of this phase is to cement this belief inside you so it becomes a fact.

You do this by feeding yourself as much knowledge as possible that supports the transformation that's taking place. The old cycle gained momentum over time with repetition, but the new cycle will overcome this power and develop its own rapidly through information. This will build the momentum behind your new cycle while in its early stages, and give your willpower the boost it needs at this time. You see, because it wasn't created by a negative experience like fear, this cycle has no bug in your web to spiral around. So you gotta make this positive one look more attractive and breaking the old one more appealing.

Don't panic, there's a lot of information out there to help you and in places you might not think to look. Apps like TikTok have short clips to give you a burst of positivity. Bite-size pieces of wisdom can be great when you're not up for an information overload. But when you are, there's more content to consume on a singular topic than you can get through in a lifetime.

So expose your mind to informative content that increases your willpower and creates an insatiable desire for success. Focus on both your old cycle *and* your new one. By doing this you protect yourself from going back whilst simultaneously propelling yourself forward! Just like you used multiple kinds of expression, get your knowledge from a variety of sources. Check out podcasts, interviews, documentaries, books, journal articles, videos, YouTube channels, blogs, memoirs and audiobooks on the subject your cycle revolves around.

What gives you the highest chance of success when breaking a cycle? Awareness. So what do you think your goal is here? Awareness. It's proven to achieve sizeable results. You already know this because you would never have been able to get to this point without it.

Any resistance or disbelief still residing in you will be met with information about where you were, where you're going and how your life will improve when you get there. You will believe that you can break the cycle because you're filling yourself up with knowledge and stories from people who already did! They put in the hard yards so you can stroll down easy street. Basically you hijack their experience and take the information from it. Then you integrate that knowledge and use it to support the new cycle in your life.

A cycle forms after a negative life experience. But you cannot break it simply by forming a positive one on top of it. If it was that easy none of us would get stuck repeating cycles because we could just rewrite over them. But what you're actually doing in this phase is connecting new mental and emotional cycles, which you need to get to the last phase where you experience the natural expression of them in physical form.

Think about it. Your thoughts stay focused on the knowledge you are gaining which feeds energy to the new mental cycle. This makes you feel the positive emotions of having achieved your goal which connects the two together and creates the belief that you can make the new one your reality. The information binds what you're thinking to how you're feeling, cementing the belief that you have the power to break it.

Now that you got your facts straight, you can finally live the dream!

Experience

To be honest, most people won't even get to the point you're at now - where they're looking for answers and are willing to put in the work. Most people just want the knowledge to be enough to pass the test without ever having to actually take it.

The new and positive cycle happening on its own is the last thing you experience when you're breaking one. It's your ultimate goal but to get here you must achieve many others on the journey. I'm not going to lie, it takes a concentrated effort over an extended period of time to master the self and free the bug from your web. As much as I wish it was, it's not a magical quick fix. It is a process that needs enough of your willpower, repetition and obsession to release the past and grasp your promising future.

Experiencing the new cycle ten times in a row doesn't mean your work is done either. Yes, you have soared through the initial challenge, but you must keep it up or else you'll just go into default-mode and repeat the old cycle. Don't get complacent because the real win is right around the corner. Stay alert and stay aware so this new experience sticks!

Being in this phase is the greatest feeling in the world. You know you've changed your life for the better and accomplished a monumental goal so you will do everything in your power to sustain this transformation.

Your Web of Life Starter Kit

Now the cycles I have shared with you are some of the most common and ones that I have been (or still am) stuck repeating myself. To be honest there are more cycles than I can possibly cover in one book, and each one of them is nuanced by our experiences and the unique traits of our personalities. So they will be different for everyone. If the examples provided here do not resonate, don't think you're in the clear. As the famous saying goes, "seek and you shall find".

You see, cycles will always revolve, that's what they do. You just need them to stop spiralling downhill and limiting your life experiences. It's time to take control! You have the power to take charge of each spiral in your web and choose which direction it goes. So stop living on autopilot and going around in circles. Instead begin to weave your web with ease and flow, knowing that this journey of self-discovery, recovery and mastery will upscale your life.

It really *is* more about the journey than the destination. You want it to be fun and smooth or else you're just dying to arrive. Based on the fact you have a comprehensive formula that's been tried and tested with a book to boot I assure you that your journey will be enormously exciting and easy compared to mine. I was all alone with no help, so I made every mistake you possibly could! I trekked solo through uninhabited jungle to clear a promising path for you. So the benefit of my journey full of pitfalls is that it saves you from falling like I did. Consider it my bonus gift to you!

Hopefully while reading this book you have had mind-blowing insights that have led to you to a deeper self-understanding than ever before. You've probably noticed some cycles in your life that keep you going around in circles too. Now you must apply your new and improved knowledge so that you can do the work required to break free of them.

As you can see everything through the Web of Life, start to observe yourself weaving closely and recognise when you're going in circles. You may not have started the cycle you're repeating, but you decide if it ends with you. Here you have all the knowledge, support and resources needed to break them for good. So it's time to get started on your journey! You can do it - I believe in you!

"Each of us is a unique strand in the intricate web of life and here to make a contribution."

- Deepak Chopra

Food for thought

What's your contribution to the collective web of humankind so far? More importantly, what's it *going* to become now that you're aware of *your* Web of Life?

I wish you nothing but sensational success that surprises you

STUFF THAT MUST STICK

- A cycle's 4mation = **experience - knowledge - integration - expression**

- 4 phases to break a cycle = **expression - integration - knowledge - experience**

Acknowledgements

Firstly, I must acknowledge **YOU.** If you're reading this, thank you from the deepest recesses of my soul for taking the time to read and engage with my book. Your contribution to making this planet more positive is the greatest gift to humanity and to me personally. I wish you all the best on your journey of self-discovery, recovery and mastery and am eternally grateful for allowing me to be a part of it. Let's expand the consciousness of ourselves, each other and the **PLANET**!

I'd like to acknowledge **Aboriginal Peoples** as the traditional owners of Country whose land this book was written on. I'd also like to pay respect to Elders past, present and emerging, and extend that **respect to Aboriginal and Torres Strait Islander Peoples** reading this book.

If it wasn't for a talented musician named Jhal Du Paul the Web of Life may never have come out of me. I must express my deepest appreciation for the months of intensive interrogation (and nights of personal frustration) that resulted in its creation. **JDP, I couldn't have done it without ya, mate!**

I must acknowledge **anyone I've ever met or known** as without all of my experiences and life lessons the philosophy contained in this book would not have been possible. A huge thank you to you all and my sincere apologies for anyone I have hurt along my journey!

A huge shout out to all my **BETA readers around the world** - your support and feedback helped me master the delivery of my content. Philip McDonald, Sharon Paul, Eva Volfson and Paul Obu. Special shout out to the **squad leader** Marie Rodrigues-Molesi!

Massive mention to **Mel Kingston** for giving me Mark Wolynn's book and a special thank you to **Melissa Martin** and **Ben Browne** for creatively collaborating with me on the **Mind Magic Resource**. The universe blessed me with you legends at the perfect time :)

About the Author

Ally Ammo is a renowned author, educator, speaker, content creator and thought leader. She has a Bachelor of Arts and a Master of Teaching degree from the University of Western Sydney, where she was the recipient of the Spirit of Enactus Award; recognising her dedication to shape values-driven leaders who make a difference in the world.

After being targeted as a teacher graduate and more than a decade of experience in the field, Ally left the profession early in her career to share her revolutionary philosophy on a global scale. She is the Founder and CEO of Web Of Life Co, a personal growth company focused on championing individuals and groups on their journey of self-discovery, recovery and mastery.

Ally is the creator of *Planet Positivity*, a YouTube channel which documents her epic adventures around the world - from jumping out of helicopters and into tombs to meeting people across 27 countries. Her travel and lifestyle channel has over 100,000 views and is now exploring content from her Web of Life philosophy. Recently she launched *A Lease on Life*, a podcast to share her knowledge, expertise, interviews with others and spark deep discussions with her audience.

Ally currently resides on the south coast of New South Wales with her partner Ben and his rag doll cat named Kimba. Originally, however, she is from the wild, wild western suburbs of Sydney, where her American Staffy, Bella, still resides.

Get your FREE PDF of the complete Web of Life philosophy!

The Web of Life PDF comes inside of a BONUS Mind Magic Resource specifically designed to nurture your personal growth and support your self-care while reading this book.

This valuable toolkit includes:

- ✓ Writing prompts to help you uncover, unpack and understand your web and your cycles
- ✓ Fun activities to master your knowledge of the eight elements, the four strands and how cycles are made and broken
- ✓ Powerful mindfulness and meditative practices for you to create, play and heal while you grow
- ✓ Artworks and creative exercises for your thoughts and emotions to free-flow, allowing you to relax as you process and finally let them go

Scan this QR code for instant access to your FREE Mind Magic Resource!

This awesome bonus booklet was a creative collaboration with digital artist Ben Browne and Melissa Martin of Mel's Art of Zen - a holistic art therapist with a background in psychology and a passion for helping people express, interpret and resolve their emotions and thoughts through creativity.

Web of Life Co have always got you covered! Be completely guided on your journey of self-discovery, recovery and mastery.

We wish you nothing but sensational success that surprises you!

ALLY AMMO

AUTHOR | SPEAKER | EDUCATOR | THOUGHT LEADER | PODCAST HOST | YOUTUBER | LIFE COACH

Ally Ammo is the best-selling author of the book Detangling the Web of Life, the transformational philosophy illuminating the 8 fundamental elements that have the power to make us and break us.

As an educator with a Master's degree, Ally has over a decade of experience teaching people of all ages and learning styles. She is adept at presenting content in engaging and animated ways so her audience is captivated and highly motivated. Her YouTube channel Planet Positivity has over 100,000 views and centres on her world travels, though Ally has also begun to expand on the content of her best-selling book. Recently she launched a podcast called A Lease on Life, so she can share valuable insights and words of wisdom with her unique brand of humour and honesty.

Ally can speak on an extensive range of topics, tailor-making every aspect of her talks to deeply inspire and connect people - to themselves and one another.

Below are her three most sought after topics:

THE WEB OF LIFE™
- The 8 fundamental elements of life
- Weaving a web of wonder vs spiralling out of control
- Why we get stuck in cycles and how to break them

THE CYCLES KEEPING YOU STUCK
- Step into your power to transform perfectionism and productivity
- How to break through the cycle of appearances and live authentically
- The hack to discover a cycle in action

THE FORMULA TO FAST-TRACK FORWARD MOMENTUM
- The secret to shift from procrastination to potent power
- The key to revealing the mysterious inner-workings of your cycles
- How to stop spiralling and start surprising yourself

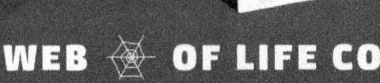

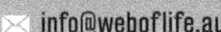

📞 0412 947 510   ✉ info@weboflife.au   🔗 www.weboflife.au   📷 weboflifeco

Awaken your Potent Power: Your Sure-Fire Strategy Session Awaits

Self-discovery, recovery and mastery shouldn't be a solo journey!

🕸 Do you feel tangled and want to free your bugs with ease?

🕸 Are you unsure of the best way to break your cycles?

🕸 Wouldn't you love a practical plan put in place to achieve your goals as *fast* as possible?

Don't miss your opportunity to personally connect with Ally Ammo! This exclusive session is designed to help you break free of limiting cycles so you can re-gain control of your life and embrace your future with newfound clarity. This transformative experience gives you the firepower to burst through the doors of lack and limitation, so you reach your full potential and get rapid, unparalleled results!

During this dynamic **Sure-Fire Strategy Session**, together we can:

- ✓ Create a customised blueprint to break your most challenging cycles.
- ✓ Uncover the big bug that keeps you going in circles, hindering your progress in health, wealth and relationships.
- ✓ Gain profound insights into your web that you cannot see clearly as the one weaving it.
- ✓ Discover powerful hacks to free your bugs, paving your way to true freedom.

Don't let life keep spiralling out of control and hold you back any longer! One quick and comprehensive chat can fast-track your path to break cycles *for good*. Reserve your spot and embark on this life-changing journey of personal growth. Spaces are limited, so get in quick to secure your session!

> * Offer available for a limited time and only valid for individuals who've read the book.

Your satisfaction is top priority! If for any reason you feel that your session did not meet your expectations, we offer a full money-back guarantee.

Results may vary based on an individual's commitment and dedication to their own journey of self-discovery, recovery and mastery.

Seize this chance to transform more than just your perspective! Awaken your potent power and transform your life. Book in now and let your **Sure-Fire Strategy Session** be the catalyst for your freedom and greatness!

Scan this QR code to check availability.

You can also watch a short video for more information about the session and check out our free resources as we're always adding new stuff.

References

[1] Lipton, B. H. (2016). *The Biology of Belief; Unleashing the Power of Consciousness, Matter & Miracles*. 10th anniversary edition. Carlsbad, California, Hay House. Inc.

[2] Daloisio, T. C., Lymanm R. K. (2017). Change the Way You Change! 5 Roles of Leaders Who Accelerate Business Performance. United States: Greenleaf Book Group Press

[3] National Scientific Council on the Developing Child. (2004). *Young children develop in an environment of relationships*. Working Paper No. 1. Retrieved from http://www.developingchild.net

[4] Rani, S. (n.d). *Basics of Educational Psychology*. Sankalp Publication

[5] Australian Institute of Health and Welfare (2022) Specialist homeless services annual report 2020-2021, AIHW, Australian Government, accessed 10 October 2022.

[6] Clinical EFT handbook Volume 1, Chapter 1, Dr Bruce Lipton

[7] Wolynn, M. (2016). It didn't start with you : how inherited family trauma shapes who we are and how to end the cycle. Penguin Books.

[8] Wolynn, M. (2016). It didn't start with you : how inherited family trauma shapes who we are and how to end the cycle. Penguin Books.

[9] Wolynn, M. (2016). It didn't start with you : how inherited family trauma shapes who we are and how to end the cycle. Penguin Books.

[10] Wolynn, M. (2016). It didn't start with you : how inherited family trauma shapes who we are and how to end the cycle. Penguin Books.

[11] Wolynn, M. (2016). It didn't start with you : how inherited family trauma shapes who we are and how to end the cycle. Penguin Books.

[12] Wolynn, M. (2016). It didn't start with you : how inherited family trauma shapes who we are and how to end the cycle. Penguin Books.

[13] Wolynn, M. (2016). It didn't start with you : how inherited family trauma shapes who we are and how to end the cycle. Penguin Books.

[14] Kox, M., Stoffels, M., Smeekens, S. P., van Alfen, N., Gomes, M., Eijsvogels, T. M. H., Hopman, M. T. E., van der Hoeven, J. G., Netea, M. G., & Pickkers, P. (2012). The Influence of Concentration/Meditation on Autonomic Nervous System Activity and the Innate Immune Response. *Psychosomatic Medicine*, *74*(5), 489–494. https://doi.org/10.1097/psy.0b013e3182583c6d

[15] Kox, M., van Eijk, L., Zwaag, J., van den Wildenberg, J., Sweep, F., van der Hoeven, J., & Pickkers, P. (2014). 0026. Voluntary activation of the sympathetic nervous system and attenuation of the innate immune response in humans. *Intensive Care Medicine Experimental*, *2*(Suppl 1), O2. https://doi.org/10.1186/2197-425x-2-s1-o2

[16] Braden, G. (2017, January 5). *Missing Links* (M. Goodson, Ed.; No. 1) [Docuseries *Cycles of Time*]. Gaia. https://www.gaia.com/series/missing-links

[17] Braden, G. (2017, January 5). *Missing Links* (M. Goodson, Ed.; No. 1) [Docuseries *Cycles of Time*]. Gaia. https://www.gaia.com/series/missing-links

[18] Braden, G. (2017, January 5). *Missing Links* (M. Goodson, Ed.; No. 1) [Docuseries *Cycles of Time*]. Gaia. https://www.gaia.com/series/missing-links

[19] Wolynn, M. (2016). It didn't start with you : how inherited family trauma shapes who we are and how to end the cycle. Penguin Books.

[20] Wolynn, M. (2016). It didn't start with you : how inherited family trauma shapes who we are and how to end the cycle. Penguin Books.

References

[21] Wolynn, M. (2016). It didn't start with you : how inherited family trauma shapes who we are and how to end the cycle. Penguin Books.

[22] Wolynn, M. (2016). It didn't start with you : how inherited family trauma shapes who we are and how to end the cycle. Penguin Books.

[23] Wolynn, M. (2016). It didn't start with you : how inherited family trauma shapes who we are and how to end the cycle. Penguin Books.

[24] Van der Kolk, B. (2015). The Body Keeps the Score: Mind, Brain and Body in the Transformation of Trauma. Penguin Books.

[25] Wolynn, M. (2016). It didn't start with you : how inherited family trauma shapes who we are and how to end the cycle. Penguin Books.

[26] Wolynn, M. (2016). It didn't start with you : how inherited family trauma shapes who we are and how to end the cycle. Penguin Books.

[27] Van der Kolk, B. (2015). The Body Keeps the Score: Mind, Brain and Body in the Transformation of Trauma. Penguin Books.

Notes

Detangling the Web of Life

Notes

Notes

www.ingramcontent.com/pod-product-compliance
Lightning Source LLC
Chambersburg PA
CBHW041316110526
44591CB00021B/2808